D1242683

Culver Public Library

WHITETAIL
RACKS

Dr. David Samuel and Robert Zaiglin

©2010 Krause Publications, Inc.,
a subsidiary of F+W Media, Inc.

Published by

krause publications
A division of F+W Media, Inc.
www.krausebooks.com
700 East State Street • Iola, WI 54990-0001
715-445-2214 • 888-457-2873

Our toll-free number to place an order or obtain
a free catalog is (800) 258-0929.

All rights reserved. No portion of this publication may be reproduced or transmitted in any form or by
any means, electronic or mechanical, including photocopy, recording, or any information storage and
retrieval system, without permission in writing from the publisher, except by a reviewer who may quote
brief passages in a critical article or review to be printed in a magazine or newspaper, or electronically
transmitted on radio, television, or the Internet.

Photos by Bob Zaiglin unless otherwise noted.

Library of Congress Control Number: 2009937526

ISBN 13: 978-1-4402-1154-6
ISBN 10: 1-4402-1154-X

Designed by Dave Hauser

Edited by Corrina Peterson

Printed in China

Dr. David Samuel
www.knowhunting.com

Dr. David Samuel spent 30 years as a professor of wildlife management at West Virginia University. During that time he taught undergraduate and graduate courses that covered various aspects of white-tailed deer biology and management. He and his graduate students conducted research on white-tailed deer, ruffed grouse, wild turkeys, woodcock, black bears, various hawks and owls, various songbirds and small mammals.

For 38 years Dr. Samuel has been an outdoor writer, with over 500 articles and columns appearing in a number of outlets. He serves as Conservation Editor, *Bowhunter Magazine* (1971-present); writes the "Know Hunting" column, *Bowhunter Magazine* (1991-present); writes the "Know Whitetails" column for *Whitetail Journal* (2005-present); and answers questions on www.sportsmansguide.com, "Ask Dr. Dave About Whitetails." In past years he has done the "White-tailed Deer" column for *Petersen's Bowhunting* (1990-1995) and also writes a weekly outdoor column in the *Morgantown Dominion Post* newspaper (2003-present).

His three latest books are *Understanding Whitetails*, Cowles Creative Publishing 1998, *Know Hunting*, Know Hunting Publications, 1999, and *Whitetail Advantage; Understanding Deer Behavior for Better Success*, Krause Publications (2008).

Dr. Samuel served on many national and state-level boards including the West Virginia Environmental Quality Board, the board of the Native American Fish & Wildlife Foundation, and the Pope and Young Club. He formerly served on the board of the National Bowhunter Education Foundation (1976-1994) and was President of that board from 1984-1988. He has been honored as the Outstanding Teacher in the College of Agriculture and Forestry, West Virginia University; received the PSE Conservation Award in 1981, the William H. Wadsworth Award, National Bowhunter Education Foundation in 1995, the Muzzy Tall Man Award in 1999, and the Lee Gladfelter Award from the Pope and Young Club, 2003. He was inducted into the SCI World Bowhunting Chapters Hall of Honor in 2001 and the Archery Hall of Fame in 2007.

In 2009, Dr. Dave received the two highest awards given to deer biologists: the Deer Management Career Achievement Award from the Southeastern Section of The Wildlife Society and the Lifetime Achievement Award from the Quality Deer Management Association.

Dr. Dave presently resides in Morgantown, WV, with his wife of 31 years, Cathy.

Bob Zaiglin
www.zaiglinswildlife.com

Bob Zaiglin serves as coordinator of the wildlife management program at Southwest Texas Junior College in Uvalde, Texas. He is also the owner of Zaiglin's Wildlife Resource Management, a consulting firm for the discriminating land steward. As a private lands wildlife biologist over the last 35 years, he has implemented management programs on over one million acres in Texas.

Bob is one of the most recognized and respected whitetail deer biologists in Texas. A certified wildlife biologist, he holds a B.S. in Wildlife Science and a M.S. in Range and Wildlife Management. His management programs have been recognized as some of the most successful in the country. Bob was awarded the Texas Conservationist of the Year by the Texas Game Warden's Association for his work with underprivileged youth hunting activities in 1985. He also received the Col. Jimmy Doolittle Award from the Buckmasters American Deer Foundation in 2002.

Bob is an official scorer for the Boone and Crockett Club, Field Editor for the Texas Trophy Hunters Association, Whitetail Deer Editor for *Texas Outdoors Journal*, and Southern Field Editor for *Deer and Deer Hunting*. His photographic skills have also been widely recognized.

As a hunter, Bob has taken two whitetails and one stone sheep in the Boone and Crockett all-time record book. More importantly, Bob enjoys fond memories of hunting with his daughters Beth and Nan as they grew up on the ranches he managed.

Bob presently resides in Uvalde with his wife of 30 years, Jan.

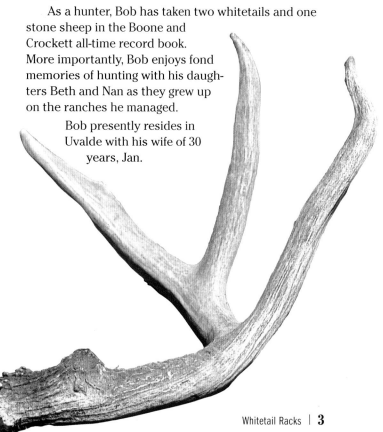

Dedication

We wish to dedicate this book to the leaders and members of the Quality Deer Management Association and the leaders and attendees of the Southeast Deer Study Group Meeting. These two organizations have done more to promote research and education on white-tailed deer than any other organizations in the country. The annual meetings of the Quality Deer Management Association and the Southeast Deer Study Group bring together the top deer scientists in the country where they present and discuss the latest in deer biology and management. Much of what is in this book either came from those meetings or from discussions with the leaders and attendees of those meetings. Our hat is off to the QDMA and SEDSG, and we thank you for what you do for the great white-tailed deer.

I, Dave Samuel, also wish to dedicate this book to my wife, Cathy, who has always supported my professional endeavors.

I, Bob Zaiglin, also wish to dedicate this book to my wife, Jan, of 30 years. Jan is not only my partner in all I do, but remains my most valuable assistant.

Dr. David Samuel & Bob Zaiglin

TABLE OF CONTENTS

FOREWORD

by Dr. Dave Samuel

As Bob Zaiglin and I were writing *Whitetail Advantage* for Krause Publications, a chapter on antlers was developed. As we covered one topic on antlers, we found another, and on and on. Very quickly we realized that there was just too much timely information on white-tail deer antlers to include in the *Advantage* book, thus, the idea for a separate book dedicated solely to antlers was born.

Every year for the past 30 years, both Bob and I attended the Southeast Deer Study Group meeting. That meeting attracts the top white-tailed deer researchers, managers, biologists, professors and graduate students in the country. These professionals present the latest research data on deer, and obviously some of those presentations involve antlers in some form or another. I also attend the annual meeting of the Quality Deer Management Association and, again, much new information is presented on antlers. This book summarizes that scientific thought-provoking information in a format and outline that we believe hunters and all deer enthusiasts will enjoy.

In addition, Bob has spent his wildlife career managing, researching and filming free ranging whitetails throughout Texas, and now continues that both as a wildlife consultant and as Department Chair of the Wildlife Management Program at Southwest Texas Junior College. I taught wildlife courses, and much of that on deer, for 30 years at West Virginia University. Both of us have written (as outdoor writers) for more than 30 years on whitetails. We've also hunted deer all our lives, representing a combined 70 plus years of experience chasing these wily and wonderful creatures.

Today we are witnessing a new era of interest in white-tailed deer. There has never been more hunter, non-hunter, and media interest in whitetails. Deer hunting remains popular. In fact, the deer hunting world is the only faction of hunting that shows growth in hunter numbers. In a recent survey done on North American hunters, when asked what species they typically hunt, 78% said white-tailed deer. The next highest response was turkeys at 23%. No question, with whitetail numbers at an all-time high, the interest is there and antlers are a huge part of the reason for that interest.

The mainstream outdoor media is inundated with discussions on antlers; how to grow them, where to find big bucks, antler restrictions, etc. Hunting television shows focus on antlers time and time again, one show after another. Deer expos focus seminars and speakers on big bucks. Some question this focus on big bucks, saying that it is not good for hunting. For some there is no question, big antlers are an obsession. For many though, taking a buck with large antlers is a goal, something strived for, something worked for, but not something that consumes them to the detriment of the resource.

Regardless of where you fit on this antler spectrum, antlers are a hot topic. In addition, quality deer management and antler restrictions are growing rapidly, leading to more mature bucks in the harvest. For example, according to the Quality Deer Management Association (go to www.qdma.org) in 1999, 2.5-year-old bucks made up 23% of the buck harvest in Maryland. That increased to 46% in 2005. Nebraska increased from 29% to 56%, Indiana from 25% to 35%, Pennsylvania from 20% to 48%. Sixty percent of the buck harvest in Mississippi is at least 3.5 years old and older. In Texas 49% of the buck harvest is 3.5 years old or older; 38% in Arkansas, 37% in Rhode Island, 28% in North Carolina and 20% in Wisconsin.

Clearly, in more and more states, it is all about antlers. The interest is there and it is intensifying. Thus, discussions on why some deer have big antlers, how to find shed antlers, why and when do they shed, how to score antlers, etc. will be of interest.

But we write this book with a little hesitancy. More and more we see a focus on trophy bucks, and there is no doubt that in some respects this isn't healthy. However, if that focus follows the guidelines of Quality Deer Management, then it can be a positive thing. Quality Deer Management involves the harvest of more does, passing up younger bucks, and having hunters as active participants in deer and habitat management. Sure, bigger bucks are a result, but a healthier deer herd and a healthier deer habitat is also a vitally important byproduct when conducted properly.

It is in that context that we write this book. The taking of a big buck with glorious antlers means little if not taken in an ethical fashion. If it is done to glorify the hunter and not the deer, it is a degrading activity. Aldo Leopold once wrote that the more you know about something, the more you appreciate it. It is our hope that readers will fulfill all the above-mentioned qualities (better management, ethical hunting, more knowledge and appreciation) once finished with this book.

As with our *Whitetail Advantage* book, we will take the basic science and latest research on antlers and put it into a book that hunters can understand and use to help them obtain greater enjoyment from deer hunting while improving their success. We know of no other book that takes the latest science on antlers and puts it in a format and verbiage for the average deer hunter. We hope you enjoy reading it as much as we did the writing.

Bob Zaiglin with a 188-inch Dimmit County, Texas, buck he took in 2000.

Dr. Dave Samuel with a tremendous deer he arrowed in Iowa. (Photo by D. Samuel)

ALL ABOUT ANTLERS

People, hunters and non-hunters alike, enjoy watching deer. They especially enjoy seeing bucks, and the bigger the antlers, the better. There is no question that hunters love seeing big bucks, but non-hunters do too. If there are four deer in a field and one is a standout, huge, big-antlered buck, he will get the most attention.

The antlers of white-tailed deer are one of the most alluring products of

Antlers are shed and regrown annually.

nature. Why is this? It could be because of the fascination surrounding their function or their formation. For instance, the only other bone cells with a comparable growth rate are cancer cells (osteosarcoma). Then there is the simple fact that they grow, are shed and lost, then regrow again. No other body part of any mammal does that. Yes, the growth rate of antlers is fascinating (see Chapter 2), but by far the main attraction to wildlife researchers and managers alike is the bona fide reverence placed upon antlers by the deer hunting sportsman.

Admiring trophy wildlife is something humans have done for thousands of years. Cave painters often used the very biggest of the species in their drawings. Based on these drawings, animals with the largest antlers or horns were the favored models. In medieval Europe, heavy-horned multi-tined red deer stags were pursued by the affluent, and mounts decorated the walls of the wealthy, in castles where these stags can still be seen today.

(below) The admiration for the largest, sometimes most dangerous, animals has existed since the beginning of time and is often depicted in paintings on cave walls.

(top) Nothing compares to the sight of a large-antlered buck, simply because those old monarchs are extremely rare.

(above) Doe harvest is increasing as proponents of quality management increase, and this represents an excellent way of recruiting young hunters.

The world is not the same as it was in medieval Europe. It's true with all aspects of our lives, including deer management and hunting. In all of hunting, perhaps the most rapid changes have occurred in the whitetail world. In recent years we've witnessed new diseases (Chronic Wasting Disease), new management philosophies (Quality Deer Management), a growth in anti-hunting, and relentless habitat fragmentation. Throw into that mix, urban deer problems and the growth in urban and suburban bowhunting for deer. Add to that the huge growth of our deer herds, and the increase in auto-deer collisions and complaints from automobile insurance companies.

(above) Antlers are often referred to as horns, but true horns, like those of pronghorn antelope, grow continuously throughout the animal's life, and cannot be replaced if damaged or broken. The outer surface of horns is composed of keratin, a substance similar to our finger nails.

(right) Although sighting deer is a cherished event, they also represent a hazard on our highways.

(below) Whitetails are extremely adaptable and do well living in areas with dense human populations.

So, at a time when state wildlife agencies are required to harvest more deer, we find (1) the anti-hunting element tying their hands, (2) state wildlife agency budgets tumbling, (3) low salaries for biologists and managers making it hard to find qualified persons to fill vacant jobs, and (4) more political interference with proven wildlife management practices.

Sportsmen now realize that they're the ultimate managers, as each time a trigger is squeezed a management decision is made.

But with all this, agencies are promoting the harvest of more deer and implementing strategies that lead to the harvest of older bucks. The 2009 Whitetail Report from the Quality Deer Management Association (www.qdma.org) presents some excellent data on changes in buck and doe harvest rates in the United States. For example, in 1999, 51% of the buck harvest in the United States was made up of yearlings. But by 2005, that percentage decreased to 45%. Our guess is that as we write this in late 2009, the percent of yearlings in buck harvests has dropped even further and we'll continue to see that trend continue in the future.

In fact, in 2008 Mississippi dropped from 50% yearlings to 12% yearlings in the buck harvest. Amazing. Pennsylvania saw a huge drop in the harvest of yearling bucks from 1999 to 2005, from 80% to 52%. Texas harvests more bucks than any other state (250,000), but only 28% are yearlings.

The function of deer antlers has been discussed and theorized by various researchers for years, but no single reason is apparent. Jim Heffelfinger discussed numerous theories about the function of deer antlers in an article in the September 2000 issue of Deer and Deer Hunting magazine.

One researcher suggested that velvet antlers dissipate excess heat during hot summer weather, but Heffelfinger rightly pointed out that if this were the primary reason for antlers, deer in the warmest climates would have the largest antlers, and they don't. Then there is the idea that antlers evolved as self-defense tools for deer. Again, there are some questions. Why would bucks then shed antlers in the winter when they are most vulnerable to predators? Why wouldn't females have antlers to help defend their fawns against predators? Good questions.

Dr. George Bubenik, perhaps the foremost antler researcher in the world, suggested that antlers function as scent-dispersers, and indeed bucks do rub trees that have scent from forehead and pre-orbital glands. And they also rub their antlers in scrapes that have urine that passed through the metatarsal gland before being deposited in the scrape. However, Heffelfinger notes that the heavily-scented velvet is shed before the rut when scent is most important for bucks.

Velvet-covered antlers have been referred to as heat dissipating organs, but if this were the case, the largest antlered bucks would be found in the warmest climates.

One obvious function of antlers is for fighting prior to and during mating season. The fact that antlers reach their maximum size right before the rut and shed them after the rut suggests that this function is very important for bucks. As we discuss in Chapter 11, some fights lead to death, but most are simply pushing and shoving matches that determine dominance. However, Heffelfinger notes that if the major function of antlers is fighting, why is there such a diversity of sizes and shapes in deer? He suggests that if fighting were the main reason for having antlers, "a single set of long spikes would be the most effective for wounding an opponent." However, he goes on to suggest that indeed all antlers are designed with sharp points on the end of each tine.

The final theory on why deer have antlers is for display. Does and bucks can visually see a deer with large antlers, and such bucks are genetically superior to bucks with lesser antlers. Or are they? Later in this book you will find that many lesser-antlered bucks mate does. However, Dr. Bubenik used mounted moose, red deer, and elk and showed that females showed more interest in the bigger-antlered males. Then there is the intimidation factor that favors bigger antlers. No question, a large-antlered buck tends to intimidate bucks with smaller antlers.

Antler size often dictates superiority among males, but not always. Sometimes it's the smaller, more aggressive buck that wins over the doe.

Regardless of function, hunters are fascinated by deer antlers. Millions of hunters travel great distances and spend much money and time pursuing this national relic we call the whitetail. At no time in the history of deer hunting, as we know it, has the demand for quality deer hunting experiences been so great. Today, the hunting experience is often measured by the size of the deer observed, not necessarily shot. Modern-day deer hunters have matured in their sport and many now search for quality rather than quantity. Accompanying this insatiable search for quality-type hunting, they are continually uncovering information on how they can reach their goal a little quicker. After all, most of us are here for a good time, not a long time.

In the past, information on deer biology seemed to elude sportsmen as it would remain ensconced in those "high tech wildlife journals." Today, readers are demanding more information on their favorite species and many of our more prominent writers have begun to inform the deer hunting public on the latest findings. Even in a market where magazines are going out of business, we are seeing new magazines devoted to white-tailed deer and antlers. They publish tons of information on deer and deer antlers. For example, studies conducted in the South show that a 1½-year-old buck has only reached 25% of its potential antler size. A 2½-year-old buck has reached 58% of its antler potential; at 3½ he has reached three-fourths of his maximum antler size; and 4½-year-old bucks have reached over 90% of their full antler potential. Though nutrition and genetics are obviously important, this data supports the assertion that letting young bucks walk is rather critical.

The most obvious function for antlers is combat between males during the breeding season.

As kids growing up, the authors couldn't wait for the only hunting magazine, Outdoor Life, to show up in the mail box. Today, a variety of magazines dedicated solely to whitetail deer exist.

The Quality Deer Management Association's 2009 Whitetail Report presents a substantial source of data on whitetail harvest. It's no secret that we've been buck-harvest oriented for years, but in 1999, that trend changed as across the country more does were harvested than bucks. That trend continues today making habitat and deer healthier. The QDMA Whitetail Report noted that doe harvests increased significantly in recent years in the Midwest. For example, as of 2005, 65% of all states were shooting more does than bucks. That statistic keeps rising every year. Delaware is number one relative to the percent of does in the harvest (70%) but Georgia, Iowa, New Jersey, Pennsylvania and Tennessee are all over 66%. Illinois, Maryland, Missouri, Ohio and Wisconsin shoot between 60-65% does in their harvests. Not surprisingly, some of these states are also key destinations for harvesting big bucks.

So read on, and discover things never published before on whitetail antlers. Our purpose is education, and we will be thrilled if you also get enthused to learn even more about our great white-tailed deer.

The whitetail is a relished sight by all, but nothing approaches the reverence deer hunting advocates place on this, the most popular big-game animal on our continent.

Few yearlings, like this youngster, are harvested in Texas.

HOW ANTLERS GROW: ANTLER CYCLES

ntlers grow faster than any other tissue, except tumors. One reason that researchers have studied antler growth is because they want to be able to treat human ailments using information found from this rapid antler growth. The antler is composed of bone, blood, and skin, so information discovered on how antlers grow might apply to the regrowth of human body parts such as fingers and toes. Sounds pretty far out, but it really isn't.

Antler growth is a yearly phenomenon that begins when they first

New antler growth is initiated annually in early spring.

erupt from the skull in late spring. But antler growth really starts earlier, about four months after the male fawn is born. For it is then that a pedicle—a bony protuberance from the frontal bone upon which antlers develops each year—begins to form. One year later the buck's first set of antlers will grow from those pedicles.

A Frenchman named Buffon published a document in 1756 wherein he stated that he believed that antlers were made of wood. Hmmm. Stick to wine my friend.

(Or maybe that was his trouble in the first place?) Wood they are not and we've come a long way in our knowledge of these bones since that time.

We don't have a lot of data from the wild on exactly when antlers start

This series of photos shows a penned two year old buck named Quatro throughout the 2009 antler growing period. The first picture (top left) was taken on April 26, 2009. (top right) Quatro's antlers on May 17. (bottom left) Quatro's antlers on May 28. (bottom right) Quatro's antlers on June 15.

to develop, but studies conducted in Mississippi demonstrated that most bucks start antler development in late April and early May. Regardless of when they start to grow, one key question is what triggers these antlers to begin to develop?

It is believed that photoperiod (in this case, increasing day length) triggers the beginning of antler growth. In fact, in the 1960s one researcher induced four different sets of antlers to grow on one sika deer (a species of deer found in Asia, but now much more common in Texas and New Zealand) in one year by simulating the natural cycle of photoperiod with artificially increased day length. He artificially increased day length and the antlers grew. He removed the antlers, waited a bit, and then repeated the procedure three more times in that same year. He also exposed bucks to equal amounts of day and night and they did not grow new antlers. Obviously increasing day length

(top left) This picture of Quatro's antlers was taken on July 7.

(top right) Quatro's antlers on July 14.

(bottom left) Quatro's antlers on August 3.

is a cue for antler growth.

Other studies show that bucks in the best nutritional condition begin antler development earlier than those on less nutrition. Although increasing day length in the spring triggers the antlers to start to grow, bucks on a high plane of nutrition will start a bit sooner than those who don't have that good diet.

Some studies show that deer on quality diets start developing antlers earlier than those on poor quality diets. One thing for certain, antlers are larger when deer obtain quality forage, which is a direct result of the right soils and plenty of rain.

Once the antlers start to develop, the male hormone testosterone controls things. We can confirm this by examining bucks that remain in velvet into the winter. When a buck is shot in hunting season with the velvet still on, he has been either castrated via some injury, or his testes have not descended. Either way, the bucks' testosterone levels are low. Higher testosterone and the velvet sheds. Lower and it doesn't (see Chapter 10).

Quatro in solid antlers with only velvet remaining (September 18, 2009)

As with all bone, growth of deer antlers is a result of two simultaneous processes. There is the formation of bone and there is also the erosion of bony tissue. That's the way it is with all bones. We are constantly rebuilding our bones. During growth phase the antler consists of a core of developing bone and cartilage covered with velvet. The antler grows at the tip, as cartilage is replaced by bone and the rate of growth is very fast. One study showed that the antler growth rate for mule deer in the early period of the antler cycle was 0.14 inch per day. By the end of the summer the growth rate slowed to 0.04 inch per day. Early antler dry matter is high in protein, but as ossification proceeds the antler is about 60% mineral and 40% organic matter on a dry basis.

It is during the early velvet stage that the developing antler is extremely sensitive and vulnerable; thus, the bucks are careful not to hurt the newly-forming structure on their heads. Injuries at this time can

inflict pain to the deer and can also cause irreparable damage to the antlers. Many of the odd points (atypical points) we observe in the fall are actually results of summertime injuries to the growing antlers (see Chapter 10). Not only are the antlers sensitive, but the rib cage also becomes fragile. Since natural occurring vegetation seldom affords a deer an adequate amount of phosphorus and calcium for antler growth, much of these required minerals are withdrawn from the rib cage. Once this occurs, the rib cage can become brittle and extremely susceptible to damage. The tips of the antlers are the last to harden, and they continue to get blood via the velvet.

Testosterone levels start to rise in late July and peak in late October. This rise causes the antler to harden and the velvet to dry up. Blood circulation to the spongy growing antler ceases and velvet shedding begins. It takes several days for the velvet to die and, once it does, the velvet becomes an irritant to bucks. They are bothered by the dry velvet and in September they will begin to rub on bushes and trees to strip the velvet from their antlers. Loss of the velvet generally occurs in one day.

The tips of the antler are the last to solidify, yet the entire antler remains covered by a protective coat of velvet throughout the summer growing period.

There is not much data that tells us exactly when velvet shedding begins, but in Mississippi the mean date was September 24th. Bigger bucks will rub trees to remove velvet, more so than smaller bucks. So a buck rub found in September is a good sign that a trophy buck lives in the area.

Once the rut is over the testosterone level in bucks begins to decline. This decline carries from December into January, and it affects antler shedding. At this time of the year we have living bone (the pedicle, the projection from the frontal bone) and dead bone (the antler). We don't know for sure why some bucks shed earlier than other bucks, but nutrition probably plays a major role (read how this works in Chapter 5).

The dynamic antler cycle in white-tailed deer climaxes when the antler, nearly seven months of age, is cast, and the new antler begins developing. Come April and May, antler growth starts all over again. Antlers are a unique happening, and there are entire books filled with research on how they form and grow. Even so, as with most of nature, there is a lot we just don't know.

Amazingly, even some of the simplest things about the antler cycle in white-tails are misunderstood by many. For instance, many people do not realize that a buck sheds and regrows

As the hormone testosterone increases in late summer or early fall, the velvet sheds away from the now solidified antler.

a new set of antlers annually. Another erroneous belief is that once a buck develops into a spike, he will remain a spike throughout his life (see

Casting of antlers indicates the climax of the antler cycle, but it's common for one side to be retained longer than the other (generally not more than a few days).

Chapter 8). Then there are some that believe a deer adds a point each year, thus one can age deer simply by counting the antler points (see Chapter 12).

As mentioned, antlers represent the most rapid bone growth known to mankind. A mature elk, for instance, is capable of growing one inch of antler per day. Growth such as this develops into solid bone sometimes in excess of 60 lbs. in under 4½ months. An elk antler of this proportion is equivalent in weight to an adult human male's skeleton. Unbelievable!!

According to Alaskan researcher Van Ballenberghe, one large-antlered bull moose in his study, whose fully-grown antlers had a maximum spread of 59 inches and a total mass of 55 pounds, demonstrated a growth rate of 14.4 oz., or 0.9 lb., per day during the month of June. This rate of bone tissue development is phenomenal and unequaled in the world.

Whether you enjoy hunting deer or simply filming them, they are something to cherish and protect for future generations to enjoy. As for those amazing antlers, what can we say? There is nothing on earth quite like them, and in the summer and early fall, nothing is more impressive than a big buck in velvet.

THE COLOR OF THE CROWN

One aspect of antlers that intrigues hunters is the color. Some hunters like the more common light or white-ivory color. Others like the antlers to be dark. The darker the better. Invariably there is a great deal of speculation on what determines the color of antlers. Why are some light-colored and others chocolate brown? Why are some ivory white and others dark gray? No one really knows, and there are no scientific studies to provide answers.

If you go on the Internet and Google "antler color in deer," theories abound. Some sound so detailed that you start to believe that they are backed by science.

But no theory has been proven; they are all speculation. Let's look at some of them.

One of the top antler researchers that ever lived speculates that antler color is caused by dried blood, left there after the velvet drops off. He also goes on further to suggest that if coloration is not caused by the dried blood, then it may be caused by a reaction between the dried blood and the sap from the trees bucks rub as they remove the velvet.

Some believe that antler color is the result of the species of brush or trees that they rub.

Other web sites have picked up on this idea and simply state that antler color is determined

These two pen-raised bucks inhabited pens with only a few mesquite trees present, yet one has light-colored antlers while the other exhibits a darker colored antler.

by oxidized blood and the local rubbed tree species that bucks rub. One site takes this idea a bit further and suggests that there is a chemical reaction between the dried blood and the sap from the rubbed tree that gives antlers their own individual variation. We are guessing that the suggestion is that the chemical reaction will vary with individual deer and different tree species, thus the color will be slightly different.

We question whether the sap from rubbed trees has a role in antler color for several reasons. First, when bucks shed velvet, they often do not have to rub the tree very rigorously to remove it. During the pre rut period, bucks rub trees vigorously, tearing the bark from the tree, so that sap will flow. But early season rubs tend to be lightly done, with no major damage to the bark, so that sap will not flow. There may be exceptions, but that is our general impression.

Second, few trees release a dark-colored sap. Yes, a light-colored sap could react with the dried blood on the antler after shedding to yield a dark color, but one would think that if bucks rub their antlers and get sap on them from the tree, it would be more concentrated in some areas of the antler and lighter in other areas. But antler color does not vary significantly from one spot to another. True, some antlers have a darker shade of color near the base, but overall coloration is not spotty in nature. Whatever the color of the antler, in general the antler has that same color all over. One would be hard pressed to picture a buck rubbing every spot on its antler the same amount over the sap on a tree.

Also, if this is what caused antler color, an individual buck might show different colored antlers from one year to the next if they rub different tree species. (Or the same color each year if they rub the same species.) Maybe this happens, but it has never been reported in

any literature that we could find.

Proving this theory about oxidized blood reacting with tree sap would be difficult if not impossible. One would need a number of fresh antlers with the velvet just beginning to shed. Then one would need to take these to various tree species and make rubs. If one tree species created one colored antler, and another tree species caused another, then we'd have some proof. It is doubtful that this could be done. Still, the antler at the time of velvet shed is not totally hardened or solid as you might imagine. The antler is hard of course, but still porous and moist, and sap may well play a role in antler color.

Others support the sap theory by noting that deer in captivity (zoos and game farms), tend to have white-colored antlers, and this is because they do not have access to trees to rub. Based on my (BZ) observation of hundreds of bucks confined in breeding facilities void of brush or containing only mesquite trees, antler color can be light as well as dark. In other words antler coloration has little to do with the vegetation or trees bucks rub.

Some attribute antler coloration to the chloroplasts in the blood during the construction of the antler matrix. As the velvet is shed, the solidified antlers are covered in blood.

Once the velvet is shed, the antlers are characteristically saturated with blood that may well contribute to their color.

The larger the antler, the greater the amount of blood and chloroplasts, equating to dark-colored antlers. In turn, smaller antler require less blood, thus the antlers are lighter in color. It's an interesting idea.

Another theory is that diet may cause the color variation. However, in one region deer will all have a fairly similar diet. But we find variations in antler coloration everywhere, so this theory is probably not correct.

One of our good friends, Charlie Alsheimer, writes for *Deer and Deer Hunting* magazine and keeps deer in a large pen for photographic purposes. Few people spend as

Some believe that the number of chloroplasts in the blood helps determine antler color. The larger the rack, the greater the amount of blood in the developing antler, thus the darker the antler. Light, smaller antlers require less blood to fully develop and this may result in a lighter-colored antler.

many hours watching deer in the field as Charlie. He speculates, as do others, that genetics plays a major role in antler color. In his book, *Whitetail – Rites of Autumn*, he speculates that there are several factors that affect antler color with the most important one being genetics. He cited the fact that he observes a number of bucks in his large pen that rub the same tree species but have different colored antlers.

Everyone wants to speculate on antler color, so we shall as well. If a buck rubs a certain species of tree, could antler color vary from one buck to the next because one buck rubs more than another? That may be a possibility, but it is sheer speculation on our part.

After the antler is shed, the sun has a tremendous effect on antler color. Most of these antlers were found only a month after they were shed and all were bleached white.

We know that shed antlers bleach very quickly in the sun and tend to be white in color. The longer they are out there, the whiter they become. But this has nothing to do with the color of antlers while on the buck. We believe that genetics probably has the greatest influence on antler color, but other factors probably play a role as well. Dr. Mickey Hellickson spends a great deal of time every year doing research on deer in the field, and looking at antlers. He notes that age may be a factor as the older bucks seem to have a better chance of having dark antlers. We agree with this theory, but mass of antlers generally increases with age, lending credence to the chloroplast theory mentioned above.

As we said at the outset, there are no data-based answers to this question of the causes of antler color variation. In truth, for most of us it doesn't matter. The color of a buck's crowning glory has little to do with our admiration for white-tailed deer

The color, shape, and size of a whitetail rack may vary, but those are the things that give an individual buck "character." Variation in antler dimensions is what draws the attention of sportsman to deer. Simply put, every set of antlers is unique, and color of that rack is just another reason we love to see whitetail bucks.

Shape, size, and color are what make each set of antlers unique. One thing for certain, a hunter preparing to shoot a buck of huge proportions places little or no emphasis on the color of its antlers.

WHITE-TAILED DEER HYBRIDS

I t is not all that uncommon to hear hunters speak about the hybrid whitetail/mule deer buck they shot. If a hunter in western Nebraska shoots a buck where the G2 tine is split on top, they often jump to the erroneous conclusion that it is a whitetail/mule deer hybrid.

But the hybrid question involves more than simple misidentification. More and more whitetails are seen along river basins further and further west, in areas where only mule deer formerly existed. According to researcher Sam Beasom, former director of the Caesar Kleberg Wildlife Research Institute, whitetails have expanded northward and westward over the last two to three decades in North America and in some

instances replaced many of the mule deer. At the same time mule deer numbers are on the decline in some of those areas. This leads to the question of whether whitetails are out-competing mule deer and taking over their range. Some hunters go a step further and question whether hybrids may be the demise of the mule deer when whitetails come on the scene. However, most biologists know that neither is occurring. Whitetails are not driving the mule deer out, nor are hybrids causing the decline in mule deer numbers. Rather, as almost

(left) Forked G2s are one of the characteristics that separate muleys from other antlered game.

(below) Forked G2s, a characteristic of mule deer, is a common occurrence in whitetails as well.

always when we see declining wildlife numbers, habitat changes are probably the reason for the expanding range of whitetails and the decline in mule deer in some areas.

Around fifteen years ago, I (DS) was bowhunting for deer near Sheridan, Wyoming. The first morning, long before daylight, my guide walked me to a tree stand on a river bottom. As the sun crept over the far mountain, I could see deer feeding in an alfalfa field above me. I'd soon realize that I was looking at both mule deer and whitetails in that field. As the sun came

(below) Irrigated agricultural crops are extremely attractive to deer, representing a valuable and consistent source of nutrition.
(bottom) Agricultural crops represent a source of nutrition throughout the West, drawing mule deer down from the high country and whitetails from the cottonwood tree-lined river bottoms in the valleys.

up, the mule deer moved up the mountain to bed for the day, while the whitetails moved my way to spend the day in the cool thickets along the river. Clearly, in that part of Wyoming though they might feed in some of the same alfalfa fields, these two species preferred different habitats.

Blacktail/Whitetail Hybrids

Deer matings can result in hybrids. It was once believed that black-tailed deer resulted from hybridization of whitetails and mule deer. However, relatively recent DNA studies show that black-tailed bucks hybridized with whitetail does to produce mule deer. The speculation is that thousands of years ago whitetails moved from the East to the Northwest coast and became a separate species, the blacktail. Later, the blacktail range expanded to the Midwest, where it

overlapped the white-tailed deer, and hybrid mule deer were the result. At least that is the speculation.

Whitetail/Mule Deer Hybrids

The first documented hybrid between white-tailed deer and mule deer was in the Cincinnati zoo in 1898. Numerous other zoos reported such hybrids over the ensuing years, but we now know that deer in the wild do, on rare occasions, hybridize. The reason that such hybridization is so rare in the wild is because there are different behavioral cues (body language, scents, what does do when bucks approach, etc.) used by both species that prevent mating with other species. We know that whitetail/mule deer hybridization is rare simply because the two species remain distinct throughout their range. If hybrids were common, and if the hybrids could successfully breed, then we'd lose the distinctive antler configuration of whitetails and mule deer. That isn't happening.

Hybrids have been reported throughout the Midwest, from Alberta to Texas. But no matter where they are found, hybrids in the wild are rare. One 1973 study found only 10 hybrids among 17,000 deer harvested in Nebraska, two hybrids out of 983 in Kansas, and six of several thousand from Alberta.

Except for parts of West Texas and Arizona, the most common pairings between these two species involves a whitetail buck and mule deer doe. Such hybridization usually takes place where the two species overlap, and it tends to happen where whitetail numbers are low. The speculation is that because whitetail numbers are low, the whitetail bucks can't find whitetail does, and being a bit more aggressive than mule deer bucks, they then mate mule deer does. Not often, but it happens. However, most hybrids do not survive. Apparently, even in captivity, most hybrids die within six months. Survival in the wild is probably even less likely, but some hybrids obviously do survive. Charles Kay, private consultant and adjunct professor at Utah State University, observed three living hybrids in Wyoming, and all were associated with female mule deer (further confirmation that mule deer does are usually involved rather than whitetail does). At another Wyoming location he saw a male hybrid with a large group of mule deer. And in a third area he noted two bucks, four does, and three fawn hybrids, and all were with a large group of mule deer.

This is a 3-year-old hybrid. WT male and MD female. The right G2 is split as in mule deer antlers. However split G2s is a common trait in whitetails as well. (Photo by Susan Lingle)

Less than one inch long and circular in shape, the metatarsal gland in whitetail deer is located below the mid point of the lower back legs.

(inset left) One of the physical differences between mule deer and whitetails is the metatarsal gland which is much longer, three to six inches in mule deer, and located higher up on the leg.

The fawns were commonly seen with a female mule deer doe. From these observations one suspects that the hybrids tend to be more aligned with mule deer than whitetails.

How To Distinguish Hybrids

The very best way to know if you are looking at a hybrid whitetail/mule deer is to examine the size, color, and position of the metatarsal gland. The metatarsal gland is located on the outside of the lower back leg. In whitetails, it is a small, less than one-inch long, circular-shaped, white-haired gland located below the mid-point of the lower back leg. In mule deer, this gland is a bit higher on the leg, and three to six inches long. The fur around the mule deer metatarsal gland is light brown. Hybrid metatarsal glands are located around the mid-point of the lower leg, are around 2-4 inches in size and have white hair.

Tail color can also be used to distinguish hybrids, but there is variation. Mule deer tails tend to be whiter in color with a black tip and much shorter than white-tail tails. Hybrid tails look like whitetail tails, but are darker in coloration, a bit longer than the normal mule deer tail and with a slight black tip. The ears of hybrids are intermediate in size between the two species. Antlers tend towards whitetails with unbranched single tines, however, the back tine tends to be taller as in mule deer. There is one other rather unique way to tell

hybrids: behavior. Dr. Susan Lingle has been watching mule deer and whitetails for many years and her work on these species has been highly enlightening. Using high speed cinematography she looked at the gaits whitetails, mule deer, and hybrids used to escape when alarmed. She found that whitetails gallop away rather quickly, while mule deer stotted. This stotting behavior has been described many times. Stotting deer take bounding leaps where all four feet hit the ground at once. This ability to bound away, takes them over rocks and vegetation that predators have to run around. So, though mule deer move away from predators more slowly than whitetails, stotting through thicker ground cover allows them to escape.

(above) Another distinguishing feature between mule deer and whitetail is the color of their tails. The tail of a mule deer is whiter in color and much shorter than that of its cousin the whitetail.

(left) The tail of a whitetail deer is larger, outlined in white with a dark center.

Dr. Lingle's work showed that whitetail/mule deer hybrids (fawns with both mule deer mothers and those with white-tailed deer mothers) did not stott nor gallop. They bounded in a behavior intermediate to both species. She further noted that even a hybrid that was 7/8ths mule deer and 1/8th whitetail still did not stott. Though the gait of the hybrids were much more mule deer, they still did not run away using the stotting behavior for escape from predators.

In other research Dr. Lingle found that mule deer can detect coyotes at further distances than whitetails. So, even though a bit slower, they get a jump start on escape. But if they cannot escape, they have another behavior that is different than whitetails. Mule deer will sometimes hold their ground and fight, while whitetails tend to flee coyotes. Mule deer travel in larger deer groups than whitetails, and this is a further advantage when fighting off predators. The old adage of "fight or flight" applies here. Mule deer cannot run as fast as whitetails, so they tend to fight, while whitetails run away rather quickly.

This carries over to the mothers of fawns. Mule deer mothers fight off coyotes that are attacking their fawns, whereas whitetail fawns are highly susceptible to coyotes as they cannot run fast when young. But come fall, whitetail fawns have grown and can run fast, and do when chased by coyotes, while mule deer fawn mortality goes up at this time of the year. Dr.

(above) Animals like mule deer dash off in bounding leaps that allows them to clear rock and brush, where the whitetail literally busts through the brush.

(right) Whitetails generally attempt to evade predators except during the rut, when they sometimes aggressively fight them off.

Whitetails often have split G2s.

(left) Fawn survival in South Texas often depends on climatic conditions. During prolonged drought, protective cover in the form of vegetation declines, and this makes fawns extremely vulnerable to predators.

Lingle then asks the question, "If coyotes catch more whitetails during summer and more mule deer during winter, which species of deer suffers higher levels of annual predation?" She goes on to note that, "In years in which coyotes focused their hunting on deer during winter, mule deer fawns suffered high annual predation rates. In years in which coyotes focused their hunting on deer during summer, whitetail fawns suffered high annual predation rates."

With differing gaits being very important in survival, it is easy to see that hybrids who fall in the middle somewhere relative to escape gait are not going to escape predators as efficiently as non-hybrid fawns.

We noted at the outset that some hunters use antler characteristics to determine whether the buck taken is a hybrid. The truth is that almost none of the "hybrids" that hunters report shooting are really "hybrids." Just because a whitetail buck has a split G2 tine does not make it a hybrid. It is just a whitetail with a split G2 tine. Actually such bucks are not all that uncommon.

When it comes right down to it, the very best way to determine if a deer is a hybrid is to do a DNA analysis. Researchers in 1986 checked out the mitochondrial DNA on a number of deer on a West Texas ranch. They found that, as opposed to other areas where hybrids came from whitetail bucks and mule deer does, in this area hybrids came from mule deer bucks and whitetail does. Interestingly, another Southwest study in Arizona showed that mule deer there were more aggressive than whitetails. Thus, it appears that hybrids have mule deer fathers in the Southwestern part of the country and whitetail fathers further North. No reasons are given for this difference.

From an antler perspective, the fact that whitetails and mule deer hybridize makes no difference. Sure, there are times when whitetail antlers may have a characteristic look found on mule deer antlers, but such bucks are rarely hybrids. And the fact that most hybrids die in the wild and few hybrids breed with other deer means that whitetail antlers are not impacted at all by the hybrid deer.

SHED ANTLERS: WHEN AND WHY?

Years ago, when I (DS) was a kid growing up in Johnstown, Pennsylvania, I remember my dad coming home from a deer gun hunt with a nice eight-point buck. However, the antlers were not on the deer. When my dad shot the buck, one antler fell off. When they went to drag the buck out of the woods, the other antler fell off. Fortunately, the first antler was found and there was no legal problem created by the drop off. But why did the antlers drop so early? Good question, and one that has been the center of debate for hunters for years.

Do all bucks living in one area shed their antlers at the same time? Is age a factor in determining when

bucks shed? Is nutrition the real cause of antler shedding? Does the same buck shed at the same time year after year and, if so, does that mean that genetics determines the date when bucks shed? Lots of questions, but are there any answers? Let's find out.

We know that those things sitting on top of male deer are antlers and not horns. Horns are never shed, and you can see horns on many African big-game species as well as our pronghorn antelope (photo below). If an African antelope has a horn broken in a fight with another animal, that horn is gone forever. Such break-

Horns, as opposed to antlers, are composed of a material called keratin.

age doesn't happen very often because horns are harder than antlers, but, once gone, that animal's position in the hierarchy is changed forever (above photo).

The terms horns and antlers are frequently used synonymously, but they are quite different. Horns are composed of keratin, a material much like the human fingernail. Antlers differ from horns in that they are bony projections that grow every summer and are shed every winter. But when and why they shed are the questions.

(above) The horns of many African species indicate their position in the breeding hierarchy, but if broken, their position in the hierarchy is severely impacted.

Interesting is the fact that antlers start to develop about the same time in April-May over most whitetail range. However, shedding times (also known as "casting") are variable. One thing we do know is the mechanism for shedding. There is a thin layer of tissue between the pedicle (bony projection of the frontal bone) and the antler. As this layer deteriorates (and it does very quickly, perhaps over a 24-hour period), the antler falls off.

(left) A number of variables impact the date when antlers are shed, but seldom are both shed simultaneously.

(below) Antler growth begins very soon after the old antlers are shed. Some believe that this new growth at the pedicle pushes the old antlers off, but this is not true.

Charles Alsheimer, writing in the March 2009 issue of *Deer and Deer Hunting* magazine, noted that bucks rarely drop both antlers at the same time. He feels that the second antler might drop a few minutes after the first, or as long as a week or so later.

The question of what causes the antlers to fall off, and exactly when they will cast, is another story and a mystery that has been bantered about for years. Some say cold weather triggers antlers to drop. Others say that a hot spell and hot weather causes antlers to drop. Some say the older bucks lose their antlers first. Some say that injured bucks lose their antlers first. Some say that nutritionally deprived bucks drop antlers first. Others say the most dominant big bucks do. The bottom line is that antlers can be found dropping off from mid December (though that is early) to early April, and as late as May in some parts of the country. We know that decreasing day length causes the testes to produce less testosterone and when testosterone decreases to a certain level, bucks shed their antlers.

Testosterone levels in bucks remain elevated throughout the rut when bucks fight and chase does. After the rut, testosterone levels begin to decrease and when it drops to a certain level, the tissue layer between the pedicle and the base of the antler deteriorates, and the antler falls off. So, the real question is, what causes the testosterone levels to drop to the required level?

Dr. Harry Jacobson at Mississippi State University looked at the casting dates for 24 individual bucks in captivity and found that, as long as the environment was the same, individual bucks dropped their antlers

The probability of both antlers falling off at the same time is increased whenever deer jump over fence lines. This makes fence lines a great place to look for those jettisoned appendages.

about the same date every year. Most varied by 1-17 days every year, but one buck varied by only four days every year. Remember, these are captive bucks that get the same nutrition in their diets all the time. These bucks were probably restricted in their movements and restricted from much fighting during the rut because they were penned. Thus, their body condition probably stayed the same after the rut, year after year. The fact that these captive individual bucks dropped their antlers on the same date each year suggests some kind of innate program within each buck that causes them to drop their antlers on the same date every year. Interesting.

Dr. Jacobson also suggested that bucks on poor diets, or those that were diseased (and thus in poor condition), shed their antlers earlier than they would if there were in good condition. Poor nutrition causes testosterone to drop, and, as mentioned earlier, when testosterone drops, so do antlers. Charles Alsheimer noted an example where a badly injured buck dropped his antlers two months early in New York, but the next year he was healed and dropped them at the normal time in early March.

Research that confirms this idea was conducted by deer biologist John Ozoga, who performed his studies in northern Michigan while working for the Michigan DNR. When he provided his study animals (in a rather large enclosure) supplemental feed, antler casting was delayed by a month or so,

(left) One theory is that age plays a role in the date antlers are shed. The older the buck, the earlier the shedding time.

(below) Penned deer studies show that if the individual bucks are put on a quality diet they tend to shed their antlers about the same time each year.

into February and March. Again, good nutrition apparently means later antler drop.

It appears that among northern deer, big and/or older bucks with the largest antlers often shed earlier than younger bucks, while in the South, younger bucks shed antlers before older, mature bucks. Research performed in the North suggested that this was due to the fact that mature bucks have a higher rank in the breeding hierarchy during the rut and this means they fight and chase does continually, which takes a major physical toll on their body. Pursuing does, not eating, and fighting other bucks are activities that reduce physical condition. Thus, when the rut ends, if these older bucks were run down, their testosterone levels would drop faster than normal, leading to casting of antlers. This seems to apply the further north one goes.

That scenario makes sense if you consider that in colder weather (which you have further north) the rut tends to be shorter and more compact than in the South. If the rut was extended, as it can be further south, then bucks would be even more run down than they already are. Even though the northern ruts are shorter, bucks there still have to deal with some very cold weather and deep snows when the rut ends. If the intensity of the rut continues for another month, northern bucks would really be in trouble. Now what does this have to do with antler shedding and the theory that in the North, older, mature bucks tend to drop their antlers earlier?

The stress of the rut and poor body condition cause testosterone to decline and, when testosterone declines the antlers drop. Since older bucks are more involved in the rut, they are physically and nutritionally beat up more than yearling bucks, so in the North, they drop their antlers first. One New York study showed that 62 percent of bucks 3½ years old and older dropped their antlers by mid December, while only 23 percent of younger bucks did.

In contrast, in the South, Drs. Marchinton and Miller and their graduate students at the University of Georgia showed that their younger penned bucks dropped antlers before the mature bucks. They proposed that "dominance rank interacts with length of the breeding season to determine the order in which bucks cast their antlers."

Another Mississippi State University penned study showed that yearling spikes dropped their antlers before yearling fork-horned bucks. We have no explanation for this except to speculate that even though the deer were in pens, perhaps the spikes were in poorer condition than other bucks.

Several researchers concluded that antler retention is a good measure of habitat condition. If the antlers drop later, those bucks live in nutritionally strong habitat. If bucks tend to drop earlier, such as mid-December to mid-January, those bucks live in poor quality habitat. Poor habitat leads to poor body condition. Since we know that testosterone levels drop when the bucks are in poor body condition or undernourished, a nutritionally poor habitat may also cause them to drop antlers earlier. We would suspect, then, that snowfalls, which limit food availability and intake, would impact the time that antlers drop. More heavy early snows would lead to earlier antler drops. In fact, studies show that further north, where snows are heavier, antlers begin to drop from mid December to late January.

Relative to good nutrition, studies show that bucks from the Midwest farm country (where nutrition is very good) don't seem to begin to drop antlers until mid January or later. Even though they

Older, larger-antlered bucks continually compete for breeding privileges throughout the rut, substantially reducing their physical condition. When such dominant bucks get run down and are in poor condition, they drop their antlers earlier than younger bucks.

rut hard, their overall body condition, though suppressed, isn't as bad as in areas with poor habitat. Thus, they retain their antlers longer.

(above) Excessive deer numbers place a burden on habitat, reducing the nutritional status of bucks living in that area, and this can lead to earlier shedding dates.

If there are hot does running around, then the bucks will remain in rut. If bucks stay in rut, testosterone levels won't drop, nor will the antlers. High doe numbers might mean that all does do not get bred during the November rut. If that is the case, then we'll have hot does popping up in mid December and rutting bucks will be chasing. This would keep their testosterone high and antlers could drop late. Of course, if there are high doe numbers, then the habitat might be bad, leading to poor body condition and early drop of antlers. Phew!! So many variables.

Also, where habitat is good, especially in farm country, a fairly high percentage of doe fawns will come into estrus and be chased by bucks in mid December. Again, this would mean that antlers would drop later. And one study conducted in Iowa demonstrated that almost 75 percent of doe fawns were bred, most during December, again leading to bucks keeping their antlers later than other parts of the country.

We are sure that individual bucks don't always read the books, so we might see bucks with antlers late or some with no antlers very early. The question of why some bucks drop early, some late, or in some areas antlers drop early or late, or in some years antlers drop early or late, is not an easy one to answer. It appears that photoperiod is the principal trigger for antler casting, but nutrition and stress can modify the time this occurs. It appears then that photoperiod, testosterone levels, condition of the buck, age of the buck, condition of the habitat, and where they live (North or South) are all factors that determine when bucks shed their antlers. There is a lot going on out there that will impact when a buck drops his antlers. Nobody said this would be easy.

Under ideal range conditions, many female fawns reach sexual maturity in their first fall. They then go into estrus following the initial rut, after the older does have been bred. Bucks will pursue these fawns and become further run down, and this impacts the date they will shed antlers.

FINDERS KEEPERS:
HOW TO FIND SHED ANTLERS

"The cool early morning spring breeze rapidly eroded away in the mid-morning South Texas sun, forcing me to remove my light jacket as I continued my search for one tremendous rack. Although I frequented this animal's domain in mid-December, I failed to get a good look at him. The contest between the two of us continued throughout the season, with the buck winning. It was now early May and I was continuing my hunt, this time without a gun as I scoured the ranch in search of his shed antlers. As this buck was able to evade me in the winter, he did again in the spring, but the time I spent looking for his sheds was rewarding to me, and my family as well."

This paragraph was written by Bob Zaiglin, my friend and co-author of this book. It epitomizes a phenomenon that is growing in this country—shed hunting. The motives for shed hunting are many, from

(below) Shed hunting for the Zaiglin family represents an enjoyable and physically refreshing outdoor activity.

(right) Locating a large shed antler in the spring adds impetus to one's hunt during the next hunting season.

a family outing, to cash for antlers, to patterning big bucks. No matter what the motive, shed hunting is booming with more people picking up those jettisoned appendages than ever before. Go to any region of whitetail country and there will be one person who is so consumed by shed hunting that all hunters in that area will know his/her name.

(above) The shed hunting event for the Zaiglin family represents quality time together.

(right) Locating the shed antlers of a particular buck is part of the puzzle when trying to figure out just what makes that animal tick.

I have such a friend in Ohio and his name is Wayne Bolton. Wayne gets a bigger thrill from finding a huge shed than he does from harvesting such a critter with his bow. Yes, you could say that Wayne is a shed fanatic. There are lots of those fanatics out there.

There are a plethora of reasons why deer hunters shed hunt, but for most the ultimate goal is the relocation of those antlers on that particular deer during the following hunting season. As with Bob Zaiglin, shed hunting is great family fun. You can take your kids and they can holler and have fun. No need to hide from the deer, or is there?

My friend Wayne Bolton looks at shed hunting a different way. He hunts sheds like he bowhunts. For example, Wayne starts shed hunting in early February, and he knows that bedding areas are great places to find shed antlers in Ohio. But Wayne will not go into bedding areas until mid-March, because he doesn't want to bump big bucks out of there that still carry their antlers. Do that and they may drop their antlers in another area where Wayne doesn't have access to look for sheds. By waiting until March, he knows that they've already dropped their antlers, so bumping

them out of the area for awhile won't impact shed hunting. Once he does go to bedding areas, he follows well-used trails and searches slowly. Antlers are difficult to spot in such thick cover, particularly in wet springs, requiring a slow, methodical search.

Wayne Bolton ("Mr. Shed Antler") would rather hunt sheds than live deer. (Photo by Wayne Bolton)

For the same reason, Wayne remains concerned about his odor. He washes often, washes his clothes often, and wears scent-free clothes and rubber boots. And he won't visit the same farm more than once per week. If Wayne is after one particular antler, he doesn't want to alert the buck that carried that rack. Less disturbance means the deer will continue normal feeding and movement patterns, enhancing shed hunting success. It's an interesting approach to shed hunting, but it works for Wayne. In Ohio he is "Mr. Shed Antler."

Another aspect that makes shed hunting a bit easier than gun or bowhunting is the fact that you don't have to get up so darned early in the morning to do it. With characteristically cool temperatures, a noon start-up time is just fine for shed hunting.

For the most part, the motives for hunting bone involve knowing what bucks survived the hunting season and the post-rut mortality season that is particularly hard on big bucks. And finding a unique set of shed antlers in a particular area often means that the owner lives relatively nearby.

Where do you look for sheds? As already mentioned, bedding areas are ideal places to search. Feeding areas may be even better. Wayne Bolton's strategy is to walk the edge of bean fields, winter wheat fields, etc., then move into the woods ten yards or so and walk the perimeter of that field again. He finds that is his best approach early in shed hunting season.

Wayne also scours power lines and south-facing slopes where the sun hits in the morning. Interestingly, Wayne finds certain hot spots for antlers on some farms. On one 200-acre farm he found 14 sheds with no matches in one small area. This

(above right) Shed hunting is a casual event that can be conducted at one's leisure any time of the day, making it extremely attractive to youngsters.

(right) Locating a particularly large set of sheds can be considered an accomplishment in itself. No one has ever said a buck had to be shot to be considered a trophy.

(top left) Often the skull of a particular buck may be discovered while searching for his sheds. By doing so, one can begin looking for another buck during the following hunting season instead of hunting a ghost.

(above) Agricultural areas are extremely attractive to bucks, as they represent a valuable and abundant source of nutrition. Such locations are great places to find shed antlers.

(left) Grain fields in late winter and early spring are also extremely attractive to does, forcing bucks to stage nearby in the event a doe recycles. This is why sheds are often found in such locations.

(top) Both antlers are not usually jettisoned simultaneously and the second antler may remain on the buck for several days, if not weeks, after the first is lost.

(above) Rodents, deer, even cattle will pick up and gnaw on antlers, which represent a supplemental source of calcium.

was a small, open, green field, not good feed and there wasn't good feed located nearby. Yet, every year this is where Wayne finds sheds on that farm.

Sometimes referred to as an adult Easter egg hunt, shed hunting is simply a harmless form of hunting.

When he finds a shed, he will make expanding circles around that location, searching for the matching antler. Sometimes that works, sometimes it doesn't. It's not uncommon to find the match a mile from where you find the first one.

Serious deer hunters devote a great deal of time each spring and early summer in search of shed antlers. But not all their time is spent picking up sheds. The fact is, shed antlers, particularly large ones, are difficult to locate. But the time afield with family and friends is rewarding in many ways other than the relocation of these calcified gems.

Each antler is unique in its own way, making it a trophy whether it is on or off the head of the animal. After all, no one ever said that a set of antlers must be obtained by shooting a deer in order to be regarded as a trophy. Thus, the search of shed antlers is simply a harmless form of hunting.

Shed hunting time is one of rejuvenation. With trees and flowers starting to bloom and exploding into every color of the spectrum, it is a refreshing time to be outdoors. Mother Nature takes on a new face. As for whitetail deer, does begin to isolate themselves in preparation for the upcoming fawning season. Bucks, however, begin to concentrate in bachelor groups and take on a new cosmetic look as they go through a most dramatic change. They cast off those antlers in preparation for the rapid generation of new ones, affording outdoor enthusiasts another excuse to venture outdoors in search of those antlers.

When searching for sheds, food plots are ideal locations to examine. Why? The answer is simple. Once the peak breeding season

(below) Springtime in the outdoors is refreshing as Mother Nature explodes into virtually every color of the spectrum.

(top & bottom) Food plots not only represent an excellent source of nutrition, but additional opportunities to locate receptive late cycling does. This forces bucks to concentrate around such areas, resulting in ideal areas to locate sheds.

(above) Areas around supplemental feed are also great places to search for shed antlers.

(left) Deer concentrate around water sources, particularly in the Southwest, where high temperatures are common in the spring. Check out those water holes, and you may be surprised what you discover.

Injured bucks often search out water. We're not sure why they do so, but it may be to escape harassing predators or assuage the acute temperature caused by infection.

(left) Fence lines force deer to jump and the sudden impact upon landing often jolts their antlers, forcing them to fall off.

concludes, most nutritionally stressed bucks station themselves around food plots to obtain a substantial amount of quality forage, foregoing the energy expenditure in search of native high quality plants following the physically demanding rut.

Another reason male deer remain around man-made food plots is to make themselves readily available to the plots' most frequent visitor, the doe. The critical factor here is that the buck is accessible to those does, even fawns, that have not conceived and will recycle. Thus, the bucks have several important biological reasons to locate near these food sources, making food plots ideal locations for shed antlers in the spring. Of the hundreds of sheds found each year on ranches managed by Bob, most will be discovered on or around food plots. If a supplemental feed is provided, these are ideal places to search for sheds, as deer concentrate around them throughout the spring.

Check out water resources. Windmills and stock tanks are not a necessity for deer survival, but are relished when available. Not only are water resources great locations to find shed antlers, they are also ideal places to recover bucks that did not survive the winter. Bucks physically injured during the rut will eventually end up near water. Never was this so obvious to me (BZ) as it was while managing a deer herd in Anderson County, Texas,

A collection of antlers can tell a story about the abundance and quality of bucks on your favorite hunting turf.

back in the late '70s. Once the sex ratio of this herd was balanced, we found more bucks perishing from injuries incurred from encounters with other bucks, particularly during the breeding season.

Remarkably, at first, I would locate a buck or two floating in one of the many lakes existing on the property. This occurrence became so common that all the lakes were checked annually to assess natural mortality. I discovered this same activity pattern in South Texas around stock tanks and windmills.

Savvy sportsmen will always check fence lines, par-

ticularly along well-known travel corridors for sheds. Bucks jumping a fence will often drop their antlers as a result of the sudden impact upon landing. Those crossing under or between the strands get tangled, only to jerk their antlers off while negotiating their way between the fence strands.

Shed antlers also make excellent rattling horns.

Seeking cast antlers in terrain attractive to bucks is critical, but paramount to success is the abundance of deer. Like hunting for big deer, you can't find sheds if few bucks exist. Thus, if buck sightings are infrequent while hunting in the fall, don't be disappointed if you discover few, if any, shed antlers in the spring. On the contrary, if you find an abundance of freshly cast antlers, then maybe more bucks, possibly transient, exist on your hunting turf than you once thought.

Shed antlers can actually tell us quite a bit about the land and the animals occupying it. For example, the cast antlers found on ranches Bob manages are analyzed as if they remained attached to their owner. The compilation of this information can be used as one indicator of the quality and number of bucks produced in a given year.

More importantly, by recording the location of the antlers, one may become more aware of those secret haunts that those super bucks, virtual Rambos of the brush, rely on to elude hunters in the fall. So don't hesitate to investigate densely-vegetated areas. You may be surprised what you find! Sheds you locate can also be used to rattle those some animals up in the winter.

The quest for shed antlers in the spring is a unique way we can pursue deer without any damage to the resource. So the next time you visit your favorite hunting turf, get out of that vehicle and walk around that leaky water trough, stock tank, or oat patch. You may be surprised to discover your best trophy. And remember, the next time you see those antlers, they may be attached to a buck of a lifetime!

I (BZ) actually hunted for this tremendous Coues deer in Hermosillo, Mexico, right where the ranch hand found these sheds. It added much anticipation to the hunt, but the buck never showed.

Ayla is a two year old retriever specifically trained by Roger Sigler to return shed antlers. (Photo compliments of Roger Sigler)

Antler Dogs:
The Ultimate in Hunting Sheds

What would add more to an outing searching for antlers than a dog? Using a dog to find sheds? Just think about that for a moment. We use dogs to search out people, drugs, cancer (yes there are dogs that can smell cancer cells on and in our bodies), so why not shed antlers?

It turns out that there are people who train dogs to find sheds. Enter Roger and Sharon Sigler who own a company called "Antler Dogs" and train such dogs in Missouri. They start training dogs that are around eight weeks old, but point out that not all dogs will become good antler dogs. The fact is, dropped antlers give off scent and a good dog can make your shed hunting success go up dramatically. However, the training of such dogs is a bit complex for us to cover here. Note though that just because your dog retrieves antlers in the back yard does not mean you have an antler dog. That just means it is a good retriever. Finding a hidden antler is different than being a good retriever. For more on this subject, and for information on training or buying a trained antler dog, go to www.antlerdog.com and talk to Roger Sigler. He is the antler dog man.

THEY ARE WHAT THEY EAT

By now any student of white-tailed deer knows that antler growth is a function of three components: nutrition, genetics, and age. The banter continues on what component, what factor, is the most important. If you are managing your land for bigger antlers, on which factor do you focus your efforts?

It All Starts With Food

For years we've heard the debate on what is the most important factor for developing good antlers. Is it nutrition, genetics, or age? Today we know that all three are important, but two things stand out. First, bucks cannot show the full potential for antler growth unless hunters let them grow older. Second, bucks cannot show the full genetic potential for antler growth unless they eat well, because they literally are what they eat.

The older we (your two authors) get, the more we look at history for answers. And history shows us that nutrition plays a major role in the development of both above-average body weights and big antlers. Dr.

(left) A healthy habitat composed of a rich diversity of nutritious and palatable forage species is one reason trophy-caliber antlers prevail in the South Texas brush country.
(right) Although drought conditions are considered a curse in South Texas, the lack of run-off (leaching) is one of the reasons the soil remains rich in minerals, providing deer a nutritious environment when timely rainfall occurs.

Val Geist tipped us off to the role of nutrition with a paper he published in the *Wildlife Society Bulletin* in 1986 titled "Super Antlers and Pre-World War II European Research." It tells a classic story on the importance of nutrition in producing some amazing red stags. This information shows that we know the science on how to create large antlers, but we may not have figured out the management methods needed.

These studies were done by Franz Vogt and published in 1936, 1948, and 1951. Vogt believed that red stags had lost their great antlers over hundreds of years due to poor nutrition. He felt that these stags had the genetic potential to produce very large, super antlers and much bigger bodies if he could supplement their natural forage diet with foods that had important nutrients.

Vogt did no breeding for large antlers, believing that the stags already had the genes for big antlers. Instead he analyzed the chemical constituents of deer antler and bone and of forage plants and agricultural forages. From those analyses he concluded that natural forages and agricultural crops were very low in certain nutrients needed to grow big antlers. He believed that the stags of yesteryear had a more favorable environment with better foods than those of today. So he pressed sesame seeds and used the oil as a basis to create a highly nutritious oil-seed cake, supplemented with

crops and natural forages. During the year he continually varied this diet to encourage his penned stags to consume large amounts of this high-quality food and the results were nothing short of fantastic. Using this approach he raised stags that exceeded world record antlers, time and time again.

Vogt started with mature red deer that weighed 396 pounds, with antlers that weighed 13.2 pounds. By the third generation (World War II prevented him from doing further research), his stags weighed 715 pounds and their antlers weighed 28.6 pounds. He had some ancient records and found that his stag weights compared favorably to the weights of stags killed in the same region in 1617. Thus, his special diet added a lot of weight to stags, but did the diet impact the size of antlers?

In 1956 a list of the 100 best 19th and 20th century European red deer was published. The antlers were scored by the Nadler system, a widely used scoring method for that time. Vogt used the same system to score his 36 stags and here is where this experiment really gets interesting.

The number one record European stag scored 229 Nadler points and the number 100 stag scored 200 Nadler points. Between the ages of 4-8 years, 35 of Vogt's 36 stags scored over 200 Nadler points. Nineteen of Vogt's stags reached eight years of age, and six of those exceeded the world record. One of his six-year-old stags also exceeded the world record. The world record was 229 Nadler points, but Vogt's two largest stags scored 247 and 242 Nadler points. Those animals had antlers that blew the world record away. Are you

starting to see why the deer farms of today can get such huge antlers on younger bucks? Today's deer farms are doing exactly what Vogt did. They combine good genetics with great nutrition to get big antlers.

In the journal article, Dr. Geist transposed the data for red stags to white-tailed deer. In other words, take the data on what the highly nutritious food did for red stags, and extrapolate what would happen if we did the same for deer. If we took a buck that weighed 198 pounds, with antlers that scored 150 and weighed 3.3 pounds, and put them on the highly nutritious feed for three generations, we'd get bucks weighing 440 pounds, and antlers weighing 9.5 pounds and scoring 200 inches.

Vogt also did one other thing with his stags. He allowed them to control harems, but he limited their breeding tenure. Thus, when winter came, they were not as run down as they would have been had he let them compete in the full rutting period. This meant that they came out of the winter in good condition, which he felt only added to their antler potential.

In Chapter 8 we'll discuss research that looked at the interaction of nutrition and genetics on antler development. That research in Texas showed a link between poor nutrition and the formation of spikes antlers. Young bucks on less than eight percent protein

(left) Big deer, like these two-year-olds, develop in breeding pens because they are under controlled conditions unlikely to occur in the wild.

(below) A buck's continual search for receptive does, along with other buck confrontations, physically drains the animal, which is often reflected in a reduction in antler size the following year.

developed poor antlers, often spikes. More recent studies done at Mississippi State University demonstrate the importance of good nutrition on whitetail antler development. These

How big those antlers will grow often depends on the date of birth and the amount of milk a lactating doe can produce. The earlier the fawn drops, the better. It all boils down to nutrition.

studies show that small young bucks, including spike bucks, grow large antlers when given a high 13-16 percent protein diet.

You can improve nutrition for deer in several ways. First and most important is the quality of the habitat. In much of the Midwest to East forests, there are too many deer and the amount of good forage is reduced. Many mature forests have little or no understory, a nutritive desert for deer. You may also see pole timber and nothing else, because there were no rotation timber cuts done over time. This creates more areas with little understory. What is needed is to use various timber improvement strategies to get better deer forage. Almost always there is a need to shoot more does to allow the forests to grow better forage and recover from

the overbrowsing that has taken place there for many years. There are several reasons to try and keep a deer herd near a sex ratio of one-to-one, and better habitat is one of them.

You can also improve nutrition by planting food plots. Done to the extreme, though costly, means you plant enough food plots

(above) Habitat manipulation in concert with reducing deer numbers ensures all deer a nutritious diet. The objective is to maximize the amount of edge, "the point where two plant communities meet." Such areas provide the most nutritious forage.

(right) Cool season food plots represent a valuable source of nourishment when much of the native forage is dormant.

to feed your deer year round. Done to a lesser extent, you plant food plots to supplement natural forage in the forests and fields. Either way the literature is quite clear on food plots. Done correctly, they create more

forage per acre than anything you can do. If you want bigger antlers, you should definitely consider planting food plots.

Supplement Their Diet

Planting food plots is more difficult in drier areas, and there you may want to consider supplemental feeding. In fact, you might want to place some supplements for deer even in areas that are not dry, to help antler growth. We've all heard of the necessity and value of high protein food, plus a diet that contains calcium and phosphorus. But bucks also need mag-

nesium, potassium, and sodium as well as micro-nutrients such as boron, copper, manganese, selenium, and zinc.

In chapter 14, we will talk about where you go to find big-antlered bucks. As noted in that chapter, one of the best places is along major river bottoms in the agriculturally-rich Midwest. Flooding rivers deposit rich soils along the banks and over hundreds of years these soils become high in calcium and phosphorus. This means that plants growing there are also high in these nutrients. Research done in Mississippi shows that the Mississippi River delta soils are high in phosphorous, and bucks there are larger than other regions of that state.

Pelleted supplemental feeds, often called protein pellets, provide protein and minerals for deer. The effect of this on your bucks, and the need for the feed for bucks, depends on the quality of your native forage. Though helpful, the use of such feed cannot replace good native forage. You definitely need the native forage, but you may also use supplemental feeds during part or all of the year to increase antler quality. One study done by the Caesar Kleberg Wildlife Research Institute in southern Texas showed that antler size of bucks on supplemental feed increased by ten inches compared to bucks on the same area that did not consume such feed. These bucks also weighed ten to twenty pounds more.

Supplemental feeding during the antler-growing season with a high protein pellet will not only augment antler size, but provide lactating mothers a stronger diet to support their progeny—those up and coming bucks.

It is a fact that larger bucks develop in the Mississippi River delta because better soils equate to an abundance of quality forage.

These data may or may not reflect what would happen if you put out supplemental feed in your area. We know that supplemental feed is more important in areas

Although supplementing a buck's diet is effective, it's also extremely expensive, in part because a variety of non-target species utilize the supplement.

of poor rainfall, as is found in South Texas where the above research was done. Although supplemental feeding is another viable drought management technique, it should not be considered a silver bullet. Yes, it can benefit deer if conducted properly, but, like sources of water, the supplement must be distributed uniformly. It's also a technique that must be in place over time. In other words, the deer must be used to the supplement before they actually need it. People often begin supplementing deer when a drought occurs when in essence that is probably too late. By the time the deer begin utilizing the feed, the harm is already done.

John Ozoga experimented with supplemental feed in a one-square mile enclosure in Michigan in the 1970s. He noted that the deer preferred natural forage and used the supplemental feed when natural forage was low in quantity and quality. He found the least use in the spring, right after snow melt when natural forage was available. Then consumption increased through the summer and fall. He found that supplemental feeding of his penned deer increased deer weight and antler size.

Many land managers who use food plots as a source of deer food use supplemental feed "as a safety net" for transition periods when crops and other forage may be low. Some use a high-protein pellet after the bucks drop their antlers, then mix that with corn during the summer, and move to all corn in the fall.

Add Salt to Taste

We see more and more hunters using mineral blocks on their hunting lands. There is a general perception among hunters that mineral licks will increase

deer body mass and antler size. A 1991 study done of 30 deer hunting clubs in Georgia found that 85 percent of the clubs felt that mineral licks helped increase antler size. In fact, as many as 50 percent felt that licks were more important for producing bigger antlers than doe harvests, food plots, or passing up young bucks. Though mineral licks may be of value, they are definitely not more important than any of those options when it comes to creating bigger antlers.

A 1992 Louisiana study looked at 42 licks that used mineral blocks. Over the next two years, body mass and antler mass of harvested yearling bucks did not differ from weights prior to the placement of the licks. This despite relatively high levels of mineral consumption. This does not mean that these licks are not useful; it just means that over those two years, in that situation, they did not increase body or antler weight.

Another study looked at natural mineral springs in northern British Columbia where deer were observed consuming water and soil from the springs. A study of 26 mineral springs demonstrated that the water and the mud were richer in sodium and bicarbonate than their surroundings. Apparently deer used the springs because of the sodium. Other studies found that animals were using natural licks to get calcium and magnesium.

We know that phosphorus and calcium are the most common minerals found in deer antlers, but antlers also contain lesser amounts of magnesium, sodium potassium, iron, zinc, and other minerals. We also know that deer accumulate calcium and phosphorus in their bones prior to antler growth, and then use these excess minerals to help grow their antlers. They also use forage to obtain more calcium, phosphorus and other minerals during the antler growth period. That's where mineral supplements come in. Providing them during the spring antler growth phase may well benefit better antler development and size. Test the soils. If they're low in phosphorus, then mineral licks, including ones that supply salt (sodium), can definitely be important for deer.

What mineral blocks should one use? Brian Murphy of the Quality Deer Management Association suggests that the blocks should contain 1.5 to 2.0 times as much calcium as phosphorus. He also notes that the licks also need salt to sweeten the bitter taste of the calcium and phosphorus so that the deer will utilize it. Start with a higher salt content, and then, as deer get accustomed to using the lick, lower the salt as much as possible.

Broken Tines

Some hunters believe that mineral composition in the antler, or lack of certain minerals, is the reason deer are more prone to tine breakage. They suggest that in certain areas of the country, lack of certain soil minerals will lead to more tines broken on bucks.

As far as we know there is only one study that looked at this question. Researchers at Texas Tech University looked at the causes for broken tines on antlers. They studied the mineral composition at various places on each antler (sheds) to determine if mineral or morphological characteristics of the antlers predisposed them to breakage. They looked at antlers with no breaks, one tine broken, and two or more tines broken, but results were inconclusive. Though the factors that caused breakage were not clear, they did have one suggestion. Humans with osteoporosis have high concentrations of aluminum. And in years when there is high rainfall there is lower aluminum in deer antlers. Thus, it might be that in years with low rainfall, there might be higher aluminum in antlers that could lead to more breakage.

Regardless of nutritional status, aggressive bucks continually confronting other bucks will break antler points, and sometimes even the main beams.

Relative to broken tines we would add a very important addition to the above suggestion. The older your age class of bucks, and the closer the sex ratio is to one-to-one, the more competition there is during the rut. More competition for does leads to more fights, and more fights lead to more broken tines. This may explain the fact that hunters in states such as Kansas see more broken tines on mature bucks as the hunting season progresses, with mature bucks showing the highest incidence of broken tines in the late season. This probably explains broken tines in bucks more than any other factor.

Rain and Antler Growth

Rain is paramount to survival for man and animal. No one realizes this more than residents of South Texas. They understand that in this semiarid region a buck's antler size depends on rainfall.

Obviously, rainfall in April and May is critical to antler development, and in 1998 South Texas had temperatures in May, June, and July above 105 degrees on 71 days. Based on this information, it's not difficult to understand why 1998 was not a dynamic antler-growing year. As if 1998 was not bad enough, 1999 was recorded as the driest year in South Texas since rainfall records were initiated, a span of over 100 years.

Landowners and sportsmen alike are cognizant of the fact that antler quality, fawn survival, and overall herd health is directly affected during drought. During drought, ranchers are forced to feed their stock hay, corn, minerals, etc. that escalate in price as a result of drought. Not only do ranchers pay higher prices for feed, many are forced to sell their stock at below average prices. This is not the trend with deer. Hunters will pay the same lease fee in good or bad years. In other words, the game on the ranchers' property is a cash crop that does not lose its value. This fact alone should be incentive enough to manage wildlife. The question then becomes what or how can we manage deer during drought?

Carrying Capacity and Population Control

As noted above, the first consideration should be to enhance food availability on a natural basis. This can be accomplished by harvesting an appropriate number of deer during the legal hunting season. Deer management is a numbers game. The land can support only so many animals — referred to as the carrying capacity. Once exceeded, the deer herd begins to suffer; that is, survival of young and old deer plummets, body weights drop, and antler size retrogresses. However, the simple fact is that habitat is dynamic.

For example, rainfall in South Texas was abundant in 1997 and habitat conditions were superb. Forage was not only abundant, it was highly nutritious as well. The reverse was true in 1998 when severe drought and elevated temperatures reduced the forage supply required by deer to the basic minimum. In other words, deer had only enough forage to survive.

The point is, carrying capacity changes with the weather. Whenever a substantial rainfall occurs, the carrying capacity is temporarily elevated. It's not long before high temperatures and wind enhance evaporation to a point that soil moisture is eliminated and plant growth comes to a halt, making it only more important to manage deer numbers so they do well under less than adequate range conditions and superb under ideal conditions. The answer again is harvest. This fact becomes even more relevant when one considers just how much a deer consumes on a daily basis. If you consider that a deer consumes four to six pounds of forage per day, even at a five-pound rate, a single deer consumes 1,825 pounds of forage per year. By removing 10 does during the season, you are conserving 9.13 tons of food per year for remaining deer. Multiply this by 100, and you have significantly contributed to the welfare of the herd. This is why an adequate harvest is so important. In a habitat like the Texas brush country that relies on rainfall, the hunter can actually compensate for forage lost during drought through population control.

In Conclusion

Providing nutrition for deer in the wild is complex. You can't just build a food plot and throw out supplemental feed and hope for the best. First focus on the habitat, natural forage, and deer density. In most locales, there are just too many deer, so lowering numbers, especially does, may be a good first step. Only then can you begin to think about improving nutrition for your deer. We know that in most whitetail country a buck reaches its maximum antler size at age 5½ years. Further south, that might be 6½, so age is another factor in growing bigger antlers. And of course, we know that genetics is also a factor, but it is the one that we have the least control over. Genetics impacts antler size and form and will determine why some bucks are larger than others even though they may be younger. However, deer must get the right feed, and must be able to survive to the right age, for the genetic component to kick in and reflect the maximum antler potential for bucks.

Antler quality remains dependent on rainfall because more rain translates into forage production. Some deer advocates go so far as to irrigate warm season food plots to ensure that bucks get a substantial diet during the antler-growing season.

A large-antlered buck is one of nature's aberrations, but its frequency of occurrence can be increased by sustaining a balanced deer herd within the carrying capacity of the land. However, genetics is also important and probably played a role in the exceptionally long brow tines on this awesome 160-inch caliber buck taken by Alaska bow hunter Dan Foster in Illinois during the 2008 season. (photo compliments of Dan Foster)

ONCE A SPIKE, ALWAYS A SPIKE?

I f you ever want to stimulate a discussion among hunters, just ask this simple question: Should we harvest spikes? The truth is that whether or not to cull spikes may be the most debated topic in hunting camps all over the country. For years this debate has raged, with the real question being whether spikes should be culled or whether they can become bigger bucks if put on good diets. The debate really centers on whether a spike is more a product of poor nutrition or bad genetics. Back in the early 1970s we saw the first real data on this question, and the two major studies yielded contradictory results. The studies were both conducted with penned deer, one study done in Texas and the other in Mississippi. Let's take a look.

In 1974 a penned deer research facility was built in Texas on the Kerr Wildlife Management Area to study antler growth in deer. This was the site of some major studies on nutrition, genetics, and spike bucks. The Texas Parks and Wildlife Department wanted "to determine if deer that developed spike (unbranched) antlers at 1½ years of age had the same potential for antler development and body weight in later years as deer which were fork-antlered at 1½ years of age."

Several studies were conducted over the years. In one of these, nine yearling spikes were fed high-protein diets ab libitum — all they could eat. They were raised beside a group of similar-aged and similarly-fed yearlings exhibiting branched antlers. Over the next three years the antlers of the spikes improved, but their body size and antler growth were less than that of bucks that were fork horns as yearlings. One conclusion of this study was there was no reason to protect spikes.

A second part of this study looked at genetics and found that it played a role in antler development. Of 26 yearling spikes, 21 had less than eight points at 2½ years of age. However, of 38 yearling fork horn

Shooting spike antlered yearlings remains an issue among hunters as well as wildlife managers.

bucks, 31 had eight or more points at 2½ years of age. Further still, the probability of a fork-antlered yearling having eight or more points at 3½ years of age was 95 percent, while the probability of a spike yearling having eight or more points at 3½ years of age was 35 percent. In addition, the antler quality of this 35 percent was not as high as the other group. Forty-two percent had five or fewer points even though they were 3½ years of age. The obvious conclusion is that spikes do not stay spikes, but based on this study, at least through the animals third year, most spike-antlered yearlings will be inferior to other similar-aged bucks as they grow older. Based on studies done since that time, we believe that it would have been interesting if the animals were followed for several more years.

Another conclusion is that deer existing on a consistent high plane of nutrition weigh more and exhibit better antler quality than those that don't. Thus, these penned deer studies demonstrated that both nutrition and genetics are important factors when it comes to antler development in male whitetail deer. This work on penned deer led most Texans to cull spikes.

However, some Texas managers did not cull spike-antlered yearlings simply because they realized that other factors can affect antler size in the young animals. One is date of birth. If a fawn is born late in a drought ridden summer it may be nutritionally deprived and develop spike antlers in its first year. In other words, there may be two types of spike-antlered yearlings, those that are nutritionally deprived and those that are a result of poor genetics.

At this same time there were many locations in the East where many yearling bucks were spikes. Clearly shooting all of them would have seriously reduced the number of bucks available to become older. Though some hunters in those locations felt that the spikes were a result of poor genetics, this proved not to be true. Poor nutrition and sex ratios that heavily favored does were problems. How, you might ask, does sex ratio lead to spikes?

Actually the answer is quite simple. When you have lots of does out there, they all do not get bred in the main rut period, and some will get bred later, in winter. A skewed sex ratio that favors does means that you will get more late-born fawns. These fawns born into nutritionally harsh conditions are behind others, and this carries over into their yearling year. Body growth takes precedence over antler growth in young developing deer, thus these late-dropped fawns tend to be spikes.

(right) Based on penned deer research conducted on the Kerr Wildlife Management Area by the Texas Parks and Wildlife Department, a buck like this nice eight-point yearling will outperform its cohorts that were spikes as yearlings, when they mature.

(below) Late-born fawns, if they even survive, will generally be spikes as yearlings regardless of their genetic make-up.

In 1978 (to 1995), Dr. Harry Jacobson worked with his penned deer at Mississippi State University to look at this spike issue. He followed antler development of more than 100 captive bucks through successive years. His results differ from those who believed that spikes were inferior and should be removed from the gene pool. Based on his findings, Jacobson believed that there was no relationship between the number of points as a yearling and the same deer in later life. He found that the spikes catch up to the yearlings at age four and was pretty much the same thereafter. Dr. Jacobson believed that nutrition was the key and he put

yearling spikes on a 13-16 percent protein diet, and in subsequent years antler growth was good.

Consider these examples from the MSU penned deer research. One yearling buck exhibited one five-inch spike and a second spike antler that had an additional second point less than two inches long. However, at 5½ years of age this same buck was an atypical Boone and Crocket deer with 24 points. In another example, a 1½-year-old spike weighed 130 pounds. On a high-protein diet, at 3½ years of age this buck weighed in at 204 pounds. He was an eight pointer with 20-inch main beams and a 20-inch inside spread.

One of the stars of that Mississippi penned-deer study was "Timbuck," who weighed 94 pounds and had

Sex ratios skewed in favor of does contribute to overutilization of native habitat as well as extended breeding periods increasing the number of late-born fawns.

two-inch spikes his first year. After being put on a high protein diet he grew to 210 pounds and had 11 heavy points as a four-year-old. He was an awesome buck.

So, now we have two contradictory studies, both done in pens, one in Texas and one in Mississippi. Which one applied to the bucks in the wild?

The answer was not simple and the debate continued. More research on penned deer was done in Texas so let's look at one more Texas study. In the late 1990s researchers at Southwest Texas State University and the Texas wildlife agency took a long-range look at whether

(below left) This deer was a spike as a yearling but demonstrated substantial antler growth through its third year in the Mississippi State University deer research facility.

(below) This buck (called "Buttons") had antlers that were barely visible at 1½ years of age, but those increased over the next two years.

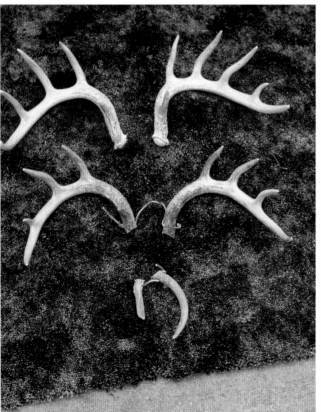

yearling spike bucks should be protected or harvested. They followed 44 yearling spikes and 100 fork-antlered yearling bucks to age 4½. All were fed 16 percent crude protein ab libitum. When the spikes reached 4½ years of age, their average Pope and Young score was 90.5. This was significantly less than that of the bucks that were fork-antlered as yearlings; at 4½ years of age they came in with scores of 127.5. When yearling spikes reached 4½ years they weighed 25 pounds less than 4½-year-old bucks that were fork-antlered as yearlings.

The researchers also presented a formula that allowed the determination of the future Boone and Crockett score of a deer based on its score as a yearling; take 92 percent of the score at 1½ years of age, add 70.5 and you get the score for that same buck when he reaches age 4½. If you take 88 percent of the score at 1½ years of age and add 61.4, you get the predicted score at 3½ years of age. In summary, this penned study showed that the scores of fork-antlered yearlings exceeded the scores for yearling spikes when these same deer were 2½, 3½, and 4½ years of age.

> **Antler size is often a reflection of habitat condition, which can be negatively impacted by burgeoning deer populations, drought, and poor domestic stock practices.**

Though the Mississippi State University work showed that spikes placed on good nutrition could develop into huge-antlered bucks, this second Texas study concluded that spike-antlered bucks continue to produce inferior antlers at maturity.

Before moving on to look at studies in the wild, let's look at a paper presented by D. F. Waldron, from the Texas Agricultural Experiment Station in San Angelo, Texas, at the West Texas Deer Study Group meeting in 2004 that might give us some insight as to why we get different conclusions from different penned deer studies. The paper was titled, "Critique of Experiments on the Genetics of Antler Traits of White-tailed Deer," and it suggested why you could get different results from similar experiments.

He felt such differences were "a result of 1) differences in herd composition in the pens, 2) differences in statistical procedures employed, and 3) differences in interpretation of results." He went on further to state that, to estimate whether genetics is an issue with spikes, you need very large sample sizes from a number of deer family units. Getting such large data sets on deer would be very difficult if not impossible.

In 2001, at the Southeast Deer Study Group meeting, researchers from Texas AM University and the Texas Parks and Wildlife agency again discussed this controversial topic. As we have just seen, previous Texas research showed that spike yearlings do not get as big when they reach maturity, even when placed on good feed. The Texas AM folks proposed three hypotheses for yearlings based on their genetic potential: 1)

that there are deer that perform well in good years (i.e. no drought) and poor in dry years (most common group); 2) that there are deer that perform poorly (relative to antler development) even on good habitat; and 3) that there are deer that always perform well.

(above) Recapturing deer on an annual basis is not only challenging but expensive. Texas researchers often employ a cannon net shot from a helicopter as it is the most efficient method of capturing deer in the low-growing brush of South Texas.

(right) Research assistants gather data including Boone and Crockett scores from all bucks they could find.

The discussion that followed was complex but showed that deer don't always neatly fit into the three categories proposed. They then made a significant point. Genetics that caused spikes and poor antlers could be masked in many deer when there was abundant food. But when you put deer on low rations of low protein diets (i.e. simulating drought conditions that are common in Texas) the bucks continue to show poor antler development.

This then leads to the simple question: How much of the antler development is genetic and how much is nutritional? The opinion of these researchers was that you can't separate the two. You need good genetics so that the bucks can reach their full antler potential with good habitat management. And for most deer, you need good nutrition to allow the good genes to be fully expressed in antler size. Finally, placing harvest selection criteria on yearlings with poor antler growth can also increase the future herd potential. (However, as you will read in Chapter 9, some authors do not agree on the value of culling.)

Now let's look at studies done in the wild. Obviously capturing and recapturing bucks year after year

The real question is if spikes breed (which some certainly do), will their progeny be spikes as well? This is a question that has yet to be answered.

Bucks in South Texas develop their largest antlers at six and seven years of age, but I (BZ) have seen them develop even larger antlers at eight to 10 years under ideal conditions, which remains dependent on rainfall.

is necessary to follow antler development, and such studies are difficult and expensive. But there have been two major studies using this approach, both done in Texas. One was conducted by in South Texas by Dave Hewitt and Fred Bryant of the Caesar Kleberg Wildlife Research Institute, and Mickey Hellickson, head wildlife biologist for the King Ranch. From 1998 to 2007, over 1500 bucks were captured on five ranches, and 377 of those bucks that were trapped as yearlings were recaptured at ages two through eight. All captured bucks were aged, weighed, and marked for future identification. There were two objectives: to determine the impact of spring rain on antler growth and to determine what happens to spikes and fork horns as they age. Do yearling spikes catch up to yearling fork horns later in life? They were also interested in comparing yearling spikes and fork horns combined to bigger yearling bucks and follow them throughout their life. For this analysis, all yearling bucks were placed into two categories: those that were spikes or fork horns, and those that had larger antlers.

At age 2½ years, 50 fork-horn yearlings had slightly larger antlers than spikes. At age 3½ years, 25 fork-horned yearlings scored six to eight more Boone and Crockett points than 3½-year-old spikes. If we just look at spikes, over the entire study, for each age class, spikes are about 15 Boone and Crockett inches smaller than bucks that started out as fork-horned bucks. But when you combine the data for spikes and fork-horned yearlings, when they reached 3½, they had antlers as big as bucks that as yearlings were six-to-eight pointers. They were similar in every respect: same number of points, same circumference, same inside spread, same main beam length, and almost the same Boone and Crockett scores.

In conclusion, the researchers feel that fork-horned yearlings will have larger antlers than spikes as yearlings, when they reach maturity. They go on to say that if your goal is to get maximum antler production, then cull out spikes. However, the authors of this work point out that there are lots of other factors to

Based on the final study, researchers found no evidence that a spike (at right) cannot turn into a quality-racked buck like the three-year-old at left.

consider before doing so: deer density, supplemental feed, fawn to doe ratio, presence of good forage, and harvest practices of your neighbors.

The question they tried to answer on rain and antler growth wasn't as clear cut. It turns out that rain/antler relationships are rather complicated in Texas. For example, the researchers found that above average rainfall in June-July and October-November led to larger antlers the following year. Even so, these researchers indicated that more research needs to be done before biologists can link higher rainfall amounts with an increase in antler size. One last gem from this study was that antler size peaked at age 6.5 years and began to decline at 8½ years of age.

The second study on wild deer was done by James Kroll and Ben Koerth from Stephen F. Austin State University in Texas. Their approach was similar to the above study. They captured bucks via aerial netting on 12 ranches in south Texas from 1999 to 2007. (All but one of the ranches was high-fenced, and the ranches ranged in size from 1200 acres to 15,000 acres.) Researchers collected various data on those bucks, released them, and then returned each year to attempt to recapture some of those bucks. They also collected data from all harvested bucks. They found that the size of the antlers in yearling bucks was a poor predictor of antler size at maturity.

Bucks that had three or fewer points as yearlings caught up to other bucks by age 4½. They caught up in the number of points, inside spread, beam length, tine length, circumference, and gross Boone and Crockett score. These authors concluded that "we believe no genetic improvement or increase in overall antler size of mature animals would be expected by culling of spikes and other small-antlered yearlings."

Interestingly, both authors of the above two studies on wild deer suggest that culling spikes outside of southern Texas is probably not a good idea. We'll talk more about this in Chapter 9, but for now it appears that in most of the whitetail world, one should give serious deliberation before implementing a program that involves eliminating yearling spikes from the herd. Habitat management which equates to nutritionally strong native vegetation is critical, and that should be a management focus.

This buck was radio-collared at 4½ and developed its largest set of antlers at 8½, when he gross-scored 188 inches.

CULLING SMALL BUCKS

Trophy bucks do not develop overnight. It takes time, patience, and for private landowners, it also takes money. As the demand for trophy-caliber deer has increased over the last 30 years, so has the involvement of scientists, biologists, and managers attempting to develop new and review old management strategies. One possible approach to getting better bucks in your herd is to cull. In Chapter 8 we covered the culling of yearling spikes, so, for the most part, what we will discuss here is the culling or harvest of older bucks exhibiting undesirable antler qualities in order to improve antler size.

The basis for culling is quite simple. It is based on the assumption that smaller racked bucks are genetically inferior, so remove them and let the genetically superior bucks mate the does. Such culling has been successful with captive herds where one can control not only which bucks mate, but also which does mate. Thus, selective breeding in captivity has led to larger antlered bucks. However, such control is obviously a great deal more difficult in the wild.

For those of you that watch the television hunting shows, you see the taking of "management" bucks on South Texas ranches all the time. They charge less for hunts where one takes a "cull" or "management" buck because such bucks exhibit what managers refer to as less than desirable antlers. To many hunters who live in more northerly whitetail areas, those so-called "inferior" bucks look pretty good. But the owners of those Texas ranches feel that their removal plays a vital role in developing better bucks with bigger antlers. And they are not alone in that belief. Some private landowners all over the country also use culls as a management tool. Does the technique work to produce better

(top left) South Texas whitetails develop their largest racks at six years of age, thus the animals must be able to survive six years on a quality diet, and this remains dependent on unpredictable rainfall.

(bottom left) Although a beautiful buck, this five-year-old eight point would be considered as less than desirable on intensively managed South Texas ranches.

bucks? That's the big question, and here is what research shows on using this approach.

Antler deformities often translate into highly desirable nontypical points, which are cherished by hunters.

Just because a buck has what appears to be deformed antlers—bucks that you might want to cull—does not mean that it is genetically inferior. As you will read in Chapter 10, many deformed antlers that look nontypical are caused after the first set of antlers begins to develop and it has nothing to do with genetics. Removal of those bucks with "deformed" racks will do nothing to change the genetics of your herd. For this reason, most culling is aimed at older bucks exhibiting undesirable antler traits, rather than those with nontypical antlers.

Then there is the theory that hunters have talked about for years: inbreeding. The prevailing discussion is that if you allow smaller bucks to breed does, you will eventually get many more inferior bucks because of inbreeding. Truth is, in the wild, the chances of inbreeding taking place is about zero and here is why. One study demonstrated that dominant bucks, ones that do a fair amount of the breeding, only stay on top for one year. One year they do some breeding, but the next year another big boy comes along and he does some. So, even if the biggest buck in your area does a lot of breeding, you won't end up with all his progeny looking like him, simply because he will only be the dominant breeder for one year.

This assumes that he does all the breeding, which brings us to the second point on inbreeding. For years we assumed that a few dominant bucks in an area did all, or most, of the breeding. Not true. In a most intriguing study done in Texas, Oklahoma, and Mississippi, Dr. Randy DeYoung disproved this belief. He used DNA testing on three different deer populations. The Texas study area was under a trophy management system where many of the bucks were over 4½ years of age. The Oklahoma study area had a number of bucks in

the 2½ to 3½ age group, and the Mississippi area had mostly yearling and 2½-year-old bucks.

Taking DNA samples of many of the deer and fawns in all three areas revealed which individual bucks mated does and the number of fawns they sired each year. Several interesting facts were learned. First, individual bucks do not mate nearly as many does each year as we once thought. Most bucks sired only one fawn each year, some sired two, and some even sired three. The occasional older buck (say, 4½ years of age) sired a few more fawns, but the average number of fawns sired by an individual buck each year was far lower than once believed.

In addition, around one-third of the fawns were sired by yearlings and 2½-year-old bucks. This was true in Texas where

Always challenged and sometimes preoccupied with a particular doe, individual bucks breed less than we once believed, regardless of the size of their antlers.

By applying modern DNA analyses, researchers proved that twin deer are not always single parented. In other words, a set of twin deer can have different fathers. More importantly this occurs more often with younger does bred by young bucks.

According to researcher Anna Bess Soren, her study included 117 fetuses representing 37 single fetuses, 37 sets of twins and two sets of triplets. Through DNA analysis, her research team attempted to match individual fetuses to the buck that sired it. Out of 37 sets of twins, both fetuses in 27 sets were confidently matched to a sire. In six (22 percent) of these 27 pairs, DNA analysis showed that the two fetuses were sired by two different bucks. The study also found that the age of the two sires were different with one buck from the oldest age class in the study (5½ to 6½ plus) and one younger buck ranging in age from adolescent to mature.

Although the number of does bred by young bucks has been proven to be reduced in Texas herds composed of a substantial number of mature bucks, the possibility of young, potentially inferior, bucks breeding could have some genetic impact on intensely managed deer herds, particularly smaller enclosed herds.

Based on behavior studies, researchers have found that mature bucks often accompany a doe over the 24 hour receptive period. By doing so, the sire prevents the doe from being bred by others. Thus a young buck would experience difficulty

> **Even if spikes are inferior, there is no way all of them can be removed. More importantly, they can and will breed.**

there were many older bucks and true in Mississippi where there were fewer older bucks. It turns out that yearling bucks do some of the breeding. Both of these points work against inbreeding. If an

> **Based on DNA research, 30 percent of the fawns are sired by yearlings and two-year-old bucks like this one. These younger bucks are available when those larger-racked older bucks are preoccupied with does.**

individual buck sires only a few fawns each year, then even if he has below average antlers he won't genetically impact the deer herd. And because so many different bucks, including the younger bucks, sire fawns in one year, inbreeding cannot occur.

If we look at just the Oklahoma data we see just how these data all played out. From 1992 to 2001, Dr. DeYoung obtained blood or tissue samples from wild bucks. He obtained the samples through live capture, hunter harvests, and shed antlers. Using 17 microsatellite DNA loci, the researchers assigned paternity to 109 of 197 fawns between 1993 and 2000. Sixty fawns were assigned to 31 known-age bucks, and 49 fawns were assigned to 16 bucks sampled by shed antlers (which were obviously unknown-age bucks). The researchers' findings indicated that lifetime reproductive success was low for most successful breeders. In fact, siring six fawns was the maximum single-year reproductive success for an individual buck. Of 60 fawns assigned to known-age sires, 58 percent were sired by bucks 3½ years old or older. Based on these findings, culling those inferior bucks does not necessarily increase the number of matings by those desirable-racked bucks permitted to remain. And since young bucks breed and there is no way to predict their antler size at maturity, another variable enters the culling equation.

One University of Michigan study revealed some interesting aspects about whitetail breeding behavior.

(left) Yearling males are socially accepted into family units primarily composed of females. Such bucks are likely to breed receptive females before being hazed away by a dominant male such as this guy, who was previously preoccupied.

(below) Twins can be sired by two different bucks, with one of the sires an older and one a younger male.

if it attempted to breed. However, in herds with tight sex ratios where many of the mature bucks are preoccupied, young bucks socially accepted into family units of does may have the opportunity to breed a young doe early in its 24 hour cycle prior to any interference by a mature buck.

How often this occurs is unknown, but in deer herds with young does representing a high percent of the female segment it may be more common than first thought.

A considerable number of Texas ranches and leases have been harvesting (culling) undesirable bucks to improve the antler quality. One question is, what bucks would be judged superior and what bucks inferior? Undesirable antler characteristics to consider when cull-

ing mature bucks include antlers lacking brow tines, short beams, lightweight beams, and a point count of seven or less at four-plus years of age. Thus, a 4½-year-old buck that has a short or no brow tines or one that has seven points would be culled. Even a 3½-year-old buck will be culled if he has no brow tines or is a small six point. These are characteristics that are relatively easy to recognize and present a good starting point when initiating a selective buck harvest.

Does the removal of such bucks enhance the bucks in your area? That is a loaded question because there are several variables that impact the results. You first need to know if the area is nutritionally stable. Genetics is only one ingredient in antler development so you must have good nutrition. A balanced sex ratio is

(above) Bucks with seven or fewer points at three years of age or older are considered undesirable and harvested as management bucks on intensive, managed Texas ranches.

(right) Mature bucks (4.5+) that gross score less than 130 inches are considered undesirable and often referred to as management bucks in Texas.

(far right) Short beams are another undesirable antler trait.

also important as is the age structure of the herd. For culling to have any affect, one needs to have at least 40 percent of all bucks over 4½ years of age. That just won't happen in the wild in many places: fenced areas, perhaps; open areas, rarely.

Old bucks with deformed antlers are less than desirable and are harvested to remove them from the gene pool.

As we learned in Chapter 8, spikes or fork-horned yearlings can attain good antlers if they get the right nutrition and are allowed to live to older ages. Thus, culling them is questionable, except in smaller high-fenced areas. That is why some ranches and leases concentrate on mature or over mature bucks exemplifying undesirable antler qualities.

Another complicated aspect to culling is the females' genetic contribution. According to Dr. Harry Jacobson, who did a lot of such research at Mississippi State University, "spike antlers demonstrate low heritability and the prevalence of this trait is more likely linked to maternal and nonmaterial environmental influences than to heritability." It is also critical to realize that there is no practical way to define a genetically desirable doe in the wild.

Most hunters agree with culling of older bucks with less-than-redeeming antler qualities. They have no problem when it comes to eliminating potentially undesirable bucks, but they also will continue to harvest bucks exhibiting desirable antler qualities, bucks that are just a tad above average. The result is a catch-22 situation—no one wins, man or deer. Remember, allowing bucks to mature is the paramount criteria in big buck production, and one of the three commandments of deer management—age, nutrition, and genetics—that sportsmen have some actual control over.

Dr. Mickey Hellickson conducted further research that throws another wrench into the idea of culling. We know that selective breeding with penned deer will lead to better antlers, but does eliminating inferior bucks in the field improve antler quality? To answer that, Hellickson took two 9,500-acre areas on the King Ranch. On one area there was similar, conservative, sport harvest of bucks. They did the same on the second site, but in addition they also harvested a number of yearling bucks with less than six points and 2½-year-old bucks with less than nine points. A total of 145 bucks were removed from the cull area over an eight-year period. Every year they recaptured as many of the bucks as they could and measured their horns. One would think that removing a number of inferior young bucks would improve the antler characteristics, but that did not happen. There was no difference in antler quality on the two areas. Hellickson attributed the results to the fact that 44 percent of yearling bucks dispersed and moved an average of 5.1 miles. You cull out inferior younger bucks and others move in from surrounding areas via dispersal. The authors of this research concluded that dispersal kept the number of

can be effective. Mickey Hellickson, chief wildlife biologist on the King Ranch supports the culling of yearling spikes, if the landowners goal is to get the biggest mature bucks possible, and understanding that you also need to take out the older "management" bucks. He goes on to note that most deer hunters will be quite happy with mature bucks that would qualify as "management" bucks in South Texas.

Bottom line, in parts of Texas, culling can and does work to improve antler quality. But outside of Texas, such management probably has little chance for success.

cull bucks the same on the treatment and control areas.

Hellickson also pointed out that the number of cull bucks on an area will vary each year depending on rain. In Texas, good rains mean good antlers. Low rains mean poor antlers. Since rains in South Texas vary tremendously from year to year, setting one standard for cull bucks will be difficult. You have to change your cull standard each year in response to the previous winter and spring rainfall.

Where does all this leave us relative to culling "management" bucks? We believe that on open range landholdings in excess of 5,000 acres in South Texas, culling is an extremely questionable method of improving antler quality. This rule of thumb probably holds for other parts of the country as well. Because of yearling buck dispersal, culling on smaller open range tracts less than 5,000 acres is also questionable. However, culling undesirable antler traits on confined (fenced) herds

(opposite) The application of a culling strategy can be effective on high fenced deer herds, but is not feasible on free-ranging deer herds.

(right) Bucks without brow tines are considered undesirable yet are beautiful.

(below) One of the major hang-ups with culling bucks is the fact that the doe's genetic contribution to the size of those antlers is equivalent to the sire, and since there is no method for selecting what an undesirable doe is, a major part of the antler puzzle remains in question.

NOT YOUR TYPICAL BUCK

Hundreds of years ago, a big nontypical deer made an Indian hunter's heart pound. The hunter of today reacts the same. In fact, nothing causes a hunter to have shortness of breath, shaky hands, and mind-numbing chills more than the sight of a big nontypical buck moving through the forest or brush, sneaking toward the hunter's stand.

Some call them "freaks of nature," but we feel that doesn't do nontypical bucks justice at all. They are grand creatures, gems of nature, which captivate us all. There is the "Hole in the Horn" buck that scored 328 points, and had a bullet-sized hole in one antler. Then there was the former world record found dead in 1981, along an interstate highway fence in St. Louis, Missouri. He scored almost 334 points. The list of bucks that hunters read about and remember goes on and on.

Where do you find nontypicals? They can pop up anywhere, but we have some information that will answer this question that you can read in Chapter 14.

Almost all of the bucks hunters see have typical racks; 3 x 3s, 4 x 4s, 5 x 5s, etc. Such racks are usually symmetrical, and thus are called "typical." But remember, being typical doesn't make them all the same. Truth is that all deer antlers are unique. One eight-pointer will have a rack that is different than other eight-pointers. It's true for each individual buck. However, nontypicals are different. Nontypical antlers are sets of antlers that do not look normal. They may have additional points at spots on the antlers where you don't normally find a point. One antler may be smaller in size. You might have drop tines coming off the main beam. You might have split brow tines. You may have "stickers" coming from one of the tines. Or in

Drop tines — points projecting downward from the beam — are extremely attractive but rare, making them sought after by deer hunters. Can you imagine walking up to this double drop?

an extreme case of nontypical antlers you may see points coming out all over the main beams. Regardless of the additional tines, a big nontypical buck is an impressive creature.

Nontypicals are rare in areas where yearling bucks make up a high percentage of the harvest. The reason is simple. Relatively few bucks in such areas live to reach 3½ years of age, and it's those older bucks that tend to be the ones that exhibit nontypical antlers. In states where harvest strategies allow bucks to get older, a buck might be a 4 x 4 eight-pointer at age 2½ years, then become a 5 x 5 ten point, but with a small drop tine on one main beam at age 3½. After that he might develop all kinds of nontypical points, and that drop tine might grow in length and width. In fact, he might well develop a second drop tine on the opposite antler, as well as some stickers coming off the normal points.

Symmetry is what best describes "typical" bucks, thus, asymmetry is a characteristic of nontypicals. T. Antony Davis from India presented a paper on antler asymmetry at the "Antler Development in Cervidae" Symposium in Texas in 1981. He suggested that the hemispheres of the Earth are bilaterally symmetrical and went on further to say that because of unidirectional rotation, each hemisphere displays certain actions that are mirror-image to those of the other hemisphere. Then he interestingly presented data on caribou and reindeer showing that this was amplified in wild animals.

For example, reindeer or caribou usually have just one brow tine and it is on either the right or left side. He looked at data from the Northern Hemisphere, from Alaska, Canada and Europe and noted that in those regions the brow tine tends to originate from the left antler. With data collected from eight Canada caribou, he found that seven had a left brow tine, none had a right brow tine and one had double brow tines. From Alaska, 17 had a left tine, six a right, and one had both. From England, 39 had a left, 25 had a right, and six both. From West Germany, 60 had a left, 37 had a right and 14 had both. The totals were 123 with left brow tines, and 66 with right ones. Apparently explorers introduced small reindeer herds in the Southern Hemisphere. On a South Georgia Island, 19 had left brow tines and 27 had right, six had both (18 had none). He concluded that these data show that there is an association between global hemisphere and antler asymmetry. We're not suggesting that the presence of one brow tine makes a caribou "nontypical," but we just found this bit of data interesting relative to our discussion of antlers.

(top) Split or bifurcated brow tines are genetically produced and extremely attractive. I (BZ) took this wide 6x7 with splits in South Texas during the rut in 1992.

(middle) This tremendous pen-raised nontypical deer is one all hunters dream about.

(bottom) Nontypical points are more commonly expressed in older bucks.

and that might lead to the nontypical points seen projecting from various parts of the skull.

(left) With matching tines on both beams, this buck's rack is referred to as typical.

That's a complicated way of saying that there are cells on the tip of the growing antler that can be moved by some type of injury. Wherever those cells end up on the skull, you may get an antler or an antler tine formed. Usually these extra tines are near the base of the antler, and grow from the frontal bone, but in rare cases, they may be as far as four inches or so from the base.

We know these extra tines or antlers can occur because of research experiments where cells were taken from the pedicle and put somewhere else on the deer's body, and this lead to the growth of a new antler. Thus, if the trauma is significant, and the tip of the pedicle is severely damaged, you might get numerous tines or a third antler formed near the base of the original antler.

Injury to the Velvet Antler

Any injury to the developing velvet antler can lead to abnormal points or growth patterns. In fact, one of the most common ways a buck can develop nontypical antlers is because of an injury when the buck is in velvet, and these injuries can be anything from a bump on the velvet, to a twig cutting it, to an insect burrowing into the velvet. But any injury to the sensitive antler at this time can lead to nontypical antlers.

Zbigniew Jaczewski from the Institute of Genetics and Animal Breeding in Poland, wrote a very interesting scientific paper ("The Artificial Induction of Antler Growth in Deer") for the Proceedings of the First International Symposium on Antler Development in Cervidae. He noted that in the old days in Europe there was intense competition among hunters to get the biggest red deer stags. Hunters learned that if you shoot stags in the velvet-covered, growing, antler with birdshot, you would get extra tine development. They did not want to kill or injure the deer, but shot them with a light birdshot to stimulate the growth of more nontypical tines. Such shooting sometimes led to the development of lots of branches. This is just another indication that damage to the pedicle area and the velvet antler early in antler development may lead to nontypical points.

Intracranial Abscessation

New research done on the eastern shore of Maryland shows that around ten percent of the natural mortality (excludes hunting) of all mature, older bucks is caused by something called intracranial abscessation. (Actually they found an even higher mortality from this disease, but suggested that around the country the mortality for older bucks from this disease makes up 10 percent of all natural mortality.) Intracranial abscessation is a bacterial infection of the brain that leads to deterioration of the skull near the pedicle and death. It is believed that any skin abrasion allows the bacteria

Injury To The Pedicle

Nontypical bucks can result from a number of causes. Sometimes there is damage at the very base of the antler. When this happens, you may get one antler growing down instead of in the normal position. Bucks have been found with a tine twisting out of the base of the pedicle and going down the side of the head. But you may also get an extra antler tine growing from another place on the skull. Here is how these pedicle injuries lead to nontypicals.

There are collagen fibers (collagen is the main protein in connective tissue) that grow in bundles at the tip of the developing antler. The antler starts to grow from the pedicle, the boney projection from the frontal bone of the skull. This growing cell mass creates tension on the collagen fiber bundles and if there is any damage when the antler starts to grow, it may move these fibers to other parts of the skull near the pedicle

to enter, and then it erodes the bone, especially at cranial sutures. Once inside the skull to the brain, an abscess forms and infection leads to death of the buck. Upon examination of a dead buck, you can often see pus oozing from the base

This buck experienced much trauma as a portion of its skull remained attached to its shed antler. If the buck survived, the antler originating at the point of damage the following year would certainly have been malformed. (Photo by Mark Conner)

of the antler or the eye socket. Upon autopsy, infection around the brain was found. In some cases, there is no visible outward sign of death, and the cause of death from the abscess is only determined by autopsy.

How and why does this happen, why is it more common in older bucks, and what do the abscesses have to do with nontypical bucks? The theory is that older bucks tend to die from this disease because of damage while fighting each other during the rut. Older bucks fight harder than younger bucks, and thus are more susceptible to skin damage. These fighting bucks put holes in the skin all over the skull. Somehow (presently unknown), the bacteria finds its way into these incisions, and then the infection process begins.

Interestingly, researchers found that bucks in the area of the study seemed to have irregular antler castings. And they noted that some shed antlers had a foul odor indicating infection. They also noted pieces of the pedicle attached to some shed antlers, indicating eroded bone that may have led to the dropping of the antler. In other words, the infection may cause part of the pedicle to break off while still attached to the antler, leading to the antler dropping before it normally would. In essence, it broke off.

Researchers noted that the disease appeared more common in nontypical bucks. They have no data to

support this idea as yet, but the idea may have merit. As noted above, damage to the pedicle can lead to nontypical antlers. Such damage can also lead to invasion of the bacteria that causes the abscess. So, it does seem likely that nontypicals may be more prone to this disease than other bucks. All of this research and the discovery of this disease in mature bucks is new, so time will tell on how the bacteria infects bigger bucks.

Body Skeletal Injury

For years we have known that body skeletal injury also causes nontypical antler development. In this situation, one antler looks normal, while the other is deformed in some way, usually smaller and nontypical in appearance. If a buck suffers a bone injury while he is in velvet, the opposite antler will often be small and deformed. This is called the contralateral effect wherein there is an injury to the back leg, and the opposite antler is affected. This happens because the nerve pathways cross over in the brain, so an injury

Often, while jumping fences, deer incur damage to their rear legs, resulting in antler abnormalities.

to the back right leg may cause the left antler to be deformed. It happens with most back leg injuries, and some front leg injuries. Note though that an injury to one side of the skull does not lead to a change in the opposite antler because nerves to the head do not cross over in the spinal cord as they do with leg injuries. Bucks hit by cars, or bucks with leg damage caused by a bullet, will exhibit this phenomenon. Any accident that seriously injures the front or back leg, shoulder or hip can lead to one nontypical antler. If the injury heals, the buck will usually develop typical antlers the following year. If not, he will remain that way forever.

(top left) There is evidence that injury to one of the rear legs causes the antler on the opposite side to be deformed. Apparently this buck injured its left rear leg while in velvet.

(middle) This buck was known to have injured himself while jumping a fence. Apparently his left side – possibly rear leg – was damaged the most.

(top right) This nontypical racked buck was taken by Stephen Mercer on the Quantico Marine Base in Virginia during the 2008 hunting season. The buck suffered from a broken left leg, which is reflected in the abnormal growth of the right side of its rack. But the buck also had very small testes, which caused him to also be a "cactus" buck. (photo by Stephen Mercer)

You can see bucks where one antler is smaller and deformed compared to the other antler and there has been no injury to the deer. However, most cases involve an injury. Let's present an example of how this may occur. We know that bucks are highly susceptible to being hit by cars during the rut. This is because they are running around, looking for and chasing does all over the countryside. If one of these bucks is hit by a car, there may be injury to the front or back leg, shoulder or hip. Since the antlers are already full grown, there will be no change to the antler. But the next year, you will see a nontypical antler develop on the side opposite of the injury. The injury that causes this is usually a broken or fractured bone. But as noted

above, if that injury heals, the next year the buck will have two normal antlers.

In 2005 a 15-year-old boy shot the highest-scoring buck ever killed by any hunter during the Iowa muzzleloader season. That buck had 38 scorable points and scored 319 4/8. This buck had a total of 162 inches of nontypical points. That is an amazing buck. Interestingly, this buck was wounded by a shotgun in the 2001 season. His antlers in 2002 showed the contralateral pattern in that one antler was much smaller

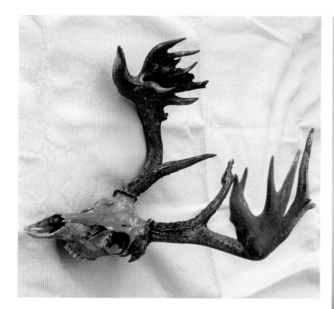

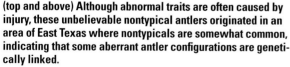

(top and above) Although abnormal traits are often caused by injury, these unbelievable nontypical antlers originated in an area of East Texas where nontypicals are somewhat common, indicating that some aberrant antler configurations are genetically linked.

(right) This world record muzzleloader buck was taken by 15-year old Tony Lovstuen in Iowa in 2005. The buck was wounded in 2001 and demonstrated the contralateral pattern in one antler in 2002; thus, the family hunting him passed him up that year. In 2003 his antlers returned to their normal, awesome pattern. With 38 measurable points scoring 319 4/8 and a total of 162 inches of nontypical points, it was truly an amazing buck! (photo compliments of Bill Winke)

and deformed than the other. But the buck healed and in 2003 he had returned to his "normal" form. He was nontypical at that time, but both antlers were of similar size indicating that he indeed had recovered from his injury.

Bioelectric Potentials

We aren't physicists, nor do we want to be, but in the book *Antler Development in Cervidae* there is a paper titled "Bioelectric Phenomena Associated with the Developing Deer Antler." Bioelectric potentials were recorded in the surface of antler tips during all phases of antler growth. Electronegativity increased as the growth rate in length increased. When they delivered cathodal direct current to the tip of the antlers throughout their development it produced abnormal branching patterns and antlers that grew in atypical directions. When they put direct current to one antler, it grew abnormally compared to its mate antler. Apparently the current retards growth at the tip of the antlers that then stimulates more growth at other locations on the antler, leading to nontypical antlers.

It has been known for years that, in humans, the application of cathodal current stimulates bone growth. With the extremely rapidly developing bone in velvet antlers, applying this current to the tip of the antler apparently stimulated growth throughout the antler, more so than at the tip, leading to nontypical growth patterns. We understand that this has no relationship to hunting, but thought it was interesting.

Hormonal Causes

Hormones control the development of antlers, and when things go awry we may get nontypical antlers. Every year you will see a published photo of a really weird buck that someone shot in the fall hunting sea-

Here is one example of a cactus buck remaining in velvet, an obvious sign that it had a testosterone problem.

Grossing 179 inches, this whopper was taken by Mike Smith in Kansas. What's really amazing is the fact that it is a doe. This was possibly the highest scoring antlered doe ever killed by a hunter. She obviously had some hormonal imbalance that led to her antlers. (Photo by Mike Smith)

son. These bucks are still in velvet and they have clusters of nontypical points, many coming from the base of the antlers. When you see a buck in velvet in the fall, you know that they have a testosterone problem, and some of these bucks in velvet appear to have a cactus coming out of their head, which is why they are often called "cactus bucks."

When a buck has small testes, or testes that have not descended normally, that condition is called hypogonadism, and it causes bucks to remain in velvet. The testes in these bucks are either gone or quite small making such bucks sterile. Behaviorally they are at the bottom of the pecking order. The reason for this is simple: they have low levels of testosterone. In the spring, as day length increases, the pituitary gland in the brain regulates other hormones including testosterone. This causes the antler to grow. In the fall, decreasing day length also impacts the pituitary and testosterone causing the velvet to shed and later on, causes the antlers to drop. Cactus bucks with small or no testes do not experience this change in testosterone levels, so the velvet stays and the antlers do not drop off. Come spring as new antler growth occurs, it grows on top and around the old antler, especially at the base, giving that weird cactus appearance. These antler points tend to stay in place in warmer climates, but further north some of these many extra tines tend to freeze and break off in cold weather. Thus, cactus bucks tend to look more unusual the further south you go.

The first thing most people assume when they see a deer with velvet antlers is that it is a buck. While that is true most of the time, there are exceptions. On very rare occasions a doe may develop hormonal problems whereby she may have both male and female reproductive organs, and this can lead to her producing antlers. Most of the time, an antlered doe only has normal female organs but still produces a very small amount of male hormones. Apparently that is possible. Regardless, most antlered does do not have enough testosterone to complete antler growth, so they usually remain in velvet and are moist. They also usually have rather small antlers.

They don't shed their antlers the normal way, but they may drop them in northerly areas where the moist antler freezes and then drops off. As with bucks, such antlered does grow new antler tissue over the old in the spring, giving them a cactus appearance.

In fact, Mike Smith from Kansas shot such a buck on December 3rd, 2008. The velvet-antlered doe had 27 points, double drop tines, and a gross Boone and Crockett score of 179 inches. This doe may be the highest scoring antlered doe ever taken by a hunter.

If a buck gets castrated while growing antlers, it not only will have velvet-covered antlers, but those antlers will not be shed. Shedding involves a decrease in testosterone, and castrated bucks have no testosterone, hence they will not shed their antlers. In a normal buck, when testosterone rises, the blood vessels going to the developing antler bone close and the velvet begins to dry and then is shed. Likewise, when the testosterone level drops in the winter, the antlers will drop off. This will not occur in castrated bucks or in bucks where the testes have not descended from the body cavity.

Genetics and Age

Antler confirmation in general is affected by genetics, but it seems that nontypical antlers are especially

Although most nontypical traits show up in older deer, this yearling buck is an exception to the rule.

(opposite) This two-year-old was nontypical as a yearling but turned into a tremendous typical in its second year, emphasizing the unpredictability of antlers.

(left) If a mature buck has missing brow tines, that is probably genetically caused. Based on what we cover in Chapter 9, this would then be a "cull" buck.

affected by genetics. There is no question that some nontypical traits in certain bucks are controlled by genetics. Antler beam palmation is one characteristic that appears to be genetically controlled, as we see bucks from one area with this characteristic year after year. If a mature whitetail buck has no brow tines, that is probably genetically caused. If a buck has very long brow tines, that too is probably caused by genetics. Drop tines are probably genetic, but they could occur from other causes. If a buck has one drop tine in one year, but loses it the next, that is probably not genetically caused. But if he develops that tine and keeps it every year, genetics most likely was the reason it was there.

Age is also a factor. The older such bucks get, the more nontypical their antlers become. This is proven over and over again on game farms where large-antlered bucks are bred to does that have sired nontypicals, hoping to get offspring that also have huge antlers. And it works. Game farmers are able to take large nontypical bucks, breed them to quality does, and get huge bucks that develop nontypical antlers. Almost surely this works the same (but to a lesser degree) in the wild.

If this is true, why don't we see nontypicals very often in the wild? Well, first we kill lots of younger bucks before they can manifest their full potential. Second, we don't manipulate genetics (i.e. control breeding) in the wild as is done on deer farms. Even if we let bucks get older, we can't

(below) Over the five-year period, this radio-collared buck didn't have kicker tines until he was 6.

Antlers progress in size with age, but when they reach those extreme ages like this old fella, antlers deteriorate in both size and shape.

do a whole lot about the does in the wild. And does contribute half of a buck's genetic makeup.

Age is also a part of the genetics equation. The older a buck gets, the greater the chances that his antlers will not be totally symmetrical. The genes for drop tines, sticker points, and extra points tend to be expressed when bucks get older. In fact, some deer biologists believe that almost half of all bucks have some genes for nontypical points. If those bucks live long enough they will develop some nontypical points. As bucks age, healthy ones increase their body and antler mass. Their antlers develop what we sometimes call "character." There are no data to support this idea, but we feel that drop tines and stickers develop on some bucks as they age and the genes for these antler characteristics are expressed.

You just don't see as many nontypical bucks in areas where yearling harvest is high. The reason is that in such areas, fewer bucks are found in the older age classes. If that is true, where can one find the most nontypical bucks? You will find nontypicals in places where you find older bucks. In fact, you will see more nontypical, older, bucks in places where the deer herd is in balance. A balanced deer herd is one with healthy does, healthy bucks, healthy habitat, and an equal or near-equal sex ratio.

As you can see, nontypical bucks arise from a number of different circumstances and conditions. Regardless of how they get there, the sight of a nontypical will stir the soul of hunters and non hunters alike. All of God's creatures are rather amazing. But these giant nontypical bucks really stir the imagination, dreams, and goals of hunters.

Regardless of how the antlers develop, seeing a nontypical like this double drop will stir the soul of hunters and non-hunters alike.

TILL DEATH DO US PART

Every year someone will post photos or videos on e-mails or the Internet showing two bucks with their antlers locked in deadly combat. Little bucks push each other around in the fall, but big bucks fight, and when they do they mean business. On relatively rare occasions these bucks will get their antlers locked. It doesn't happen often, but when it does, death is usually the result.

The pursuit of trophy deer in the brush country of South Texas during the month of December is considered by many to be the ultimate experience. As the temperature drops in December and those mature, characteristically reclusive bucks, "high on testosterone," intensify their quest for doe in estrus, they allow themselves to become vulnerable.

As the wildlife manager of a 106,000-acre ranch right in the middle of the famed golden triangle for 21 years, I (BZ) was privileged to see much of what this biodiverse region had to offer. As a deer biologist I witnessed it all, from coyotes encircling a helpless whitetail stuck in the gummy substrate of a stock tank to some of the most vicious fights between bucks imaginable. And over the years I have seen few of those combatants locked in death, that is until I accomplished one of my management objectives and balanced the sex ratio on the ranch in 1987.

Throughout the 1980s and into the 1990s, the owners of *North American Whitetail* magazine – Steve Vaughn, David Morris, and Chuck Larsen – hunted annually with me and shot some of the finest whitetails in existence, several of which grace the pages of the

The battle between two mature bucks is a knock down-drag out event, making it one of the most fascinating events a hunter can witness in the wild.

(left) With ears laid back, the bucks size each other up, characteristically changing chameleon-like, to a dark, wet chocolate color (obvious in the deer on the left) as the hair on the back of their necks stands erect.

(bottom left) Most confrontations remain as bluffs by both competitors, but once the decision to fight is made the antlers are often gingerly placed together. In this case it was abrupt, initiating a major pushing match.

(below) The sound of clashing antlers resonating into the forest or brush is extremely attractive to other bucks. I (BZ) believe that satellite bucks approach in order to steal away with the now available doe, while the two combatants fight.

Boone and Crockett record book. Indeed, many of those bucks appeared on the cover of *North American Whitetail* magazine.

On March 5, 1987, nine months before Chuck arrived on this 1987 hunt, one of the Texas Tech graduate students working on the ranch picked up a mortality signal from one of the 25 mature bucks we were monitoring for research purposes. Assisting the young man, we discovered not one, but two dead deer locked antler-to-antler. What was so impressive about this occurrence is the fact that we had only 25 bucks collared. What were the odds that one of our study animals would become locked up with another buck? Well, based on the fact that 25 bucks were collared, the probability of one locking up with another buck is one out of 25, or four percent.

When Chuck and his wife Jean arrived at the ranch, we told them about the locked bucks. Little did we know that something unique was about to happen. On December 10, 1987, Chuck, accompanied by his wife Jean and guide Tim Brooks, were on the third day of their hunt. A discretionary hunter, Chuck had already

(top left) Physical confrontations between bucks often last less than a minute or two. In this case neither buck would relinquish ground, thus the fight endured for close to two minutes.

(top right) Without observing a doe, the satellite buck remains because if one of the combatants is injured, he may join in to help the victor haze the loser.

(above left) The buck on the right loses its footing, which is an indication of weakness.

(above right) Regaining its balance, the buck that slipped early continues to fight more intensively than before, but within two minutes the battle ends as the weaker buck dashes off.

This is the first pair of bucks we found on the 106,000-acre ranch. We found these together in mid-March 1987. Both were dead and virtually consumed by coyotes. Finding a pair of bucks locked together is rare, but what makes this event most unique was the fact that one of the combatants was one of 25 bucks radio-collared in October of 1987 as part of a radio telemetry study.

(right) Each radio transmitter contained a mortality sensor that went off whenever a deer failed to move for eight hours. Without the use of the telemetry receiver, we would never have found these bucks or known they locked up.

(below) On December 10, 1987, hunter Chuck Larsen spotted these two bucks locked together as he hunted from a top-drive rig. He actually thought he saw a huge nontypical partially hidden in the dense vegetation paralleling the road he traveled. Can you imagine what he thought when he approached the two magnificent animals and discovered that one was already dead?

passed on several bucks in the 160-inch range, gambling that he would find something better, but there was no way to envision what he was about to see on that cloudy, cold December morning.

As the trio negotiated the deep red, sandy roads throughout the ranch on a top-drive rig, deer sightings were abundant, but as they closed the distance towards one of the ranch windmills, the rig came to a halt as they spotted what initially appeared to be a huge nontypical standing stationary and partially hidden in the brush along the side of the road. Upon stalking up for a possible shot Chuck discovered that it was not a nontypical-racked buck, but two huge bucks locked together with one of the gladiators partially consumed by marauding coyotes. Imagine the trauma the survivor experienced as coyotes tore away flesh from the dead buck. Nature indeed can be cruel.

Once I received a radio call from Tim I rapidly covered the two miles to the site and, with his help, we freed the lone survivor, but not before radio-collaring the deer (that gross scored 171") with a collar unused during an ongoing telemetry study we were conduct-

The burden of being attached to a dead opponent had to be stressful, but one can only imagine how much more stressful it was to avoid the coyotes as they tore away the dead buck.

ing. Amazingly, the emaciated animal dashed off into the ocean of brush only to be recovered the following morning, apparently killed by the relentless coyotes.

Unquestionably one of the rarest occurrences in the whitetail world, locating a pair of bucks entangled by their antlers with one of the combatants alive is truly phenomenal. However, 47 days later on January 26, 1988, I received a call from our ranch foreman informing me that he discovered two large whitetails locked together with one of the animals still alive. Within minutes I arrived at the scene, snapped a few photographs, and attempted to separate the animals. It was obvious that they'd been locked up for quite a long time as the lone survivor was extremely emaciated while its combatant was almost completely consumed by coyotes. Still, we worked hard to try and free the survivor. Before we were able to accomplish the task, he succumbed.

Bucks locked in death are extremely rare, but to find three pair of bucks locked together in such a short time span can be considered almost unbelievable. And when you consider the size of the ranch, 106,000 acres, it almost seems impossible. However, we managed to maintain the sex ratio as equal as possible, and also protected the younger bucks. When you do this, competition for does intensifies, as it should in a natural environment. With competition for the does, you get more fighting; and with more fighting, you get more locked bucks.

As we said at the outset, every year there are photos and stories of locked bucks. Here is one from Mel Schille, Manager with the Canadian Pacific Railway. He is now retired and a resident of British Columbia, but he lived in Wilkie, Saskatchewan, at the time. Here is his story.

It was November 9th and the train was on it's way to Lloydminster, on the border between Saskatchewan and Alberta. About 50 miles from Lloydminster, they spotted two locked bucks in a coulee, "fighting a great battle, shoving and throwing each other about. We stopped the train and watched for about 20 minutes." On the way back from Lloydminster that night, they did not see the bucks.

The next day Mel and his father, grandfather, brother, wife, and daughter drove to the area to look for the bucks. After walking one-quarter mile they heard them fighting. The locked bucks were laying down when Mel and his family first spotted them, and the bucks jumped up and started throwing each other around

(right) Initially, the surviving buck was so worn down and emaciated it allowed me to approach within a few feet before making any attempt to escape.

(far right) Although the lone survivor appeared oblivious to all around him, that instantly changed when I attempted to untangle the animals after a radio-collar was placed around its neck. It didn't take long for me to realize that I required assistance in conducting this dangerous task.

(left) Freed and wearing a radio collar equipped with a mortality sensor, the buck dashed off into an ocean of brush.

(below) Although the freed buck appeared to run off in good health, the mortality sensor went off the following morning, leading us to what little remained of the buck after falling prey to the coyotes.

again. Both bucks looked to be in good shape except for a bloody nose on one animal. They followed the bucks as they pushed each other down an embankment, up another, and down a steep hill into a fence. "At this point Dad and I pinned both deer against the fence and removed one tine . . . the end of the left antler of the deer on the right." They then cut the fence and the deer rolled into an open area, however, they were still locked together. For a second time Mel approached the deer with a wood saw in his hand. The deer did not move and Mel removed a second tine. The deer were then free, and ran off.

In Mel's letter to me (DS), he notes an appendum to this story. "Two weeks later, when deer season was open (it was closed when I cut the antlers) I was in Lloydminster sitting in a restaurant having coffee when two wildlife officers came in and sat behind me. I overheard their conversation about a hunter reporting to them that he had shot a deer in the valley and it looked like a tine was cut off. I turned to them and told them the story, but they did not believe me. I then took them down to the railroad station and showed them the pictures. They gave me the phone number for the hunter and I contacted him and sent him the tines that I had removed as I still had them." What are the chances of that happening?

There are no data on how often such fighting occurs in whitetails, nor how many bucks that get locked actually die. There is one published study on Russian red stags found dead in the field, and 13 percent died of wounds received in fights. In another study done on Scottish red stags, 25 percent had signs of damage and

six percent suffered permanent injuries from fighting in one year.

The antlers of a deer are shaped to do damage to other deer. Yes, they can use them to defend against predators (wolves, coyotes, mountain lions, bobcats), but for the most part deer use their antlers against other deer. And as we have seen from the above stories and data, it can get pretty serious. Dr. Val Geist conducted an interesting study that shows just how much damage antlered species do to each other.

Dr. Geist tracked down the hides of moose, white-tailed deer, mule deer, and elk, and examined them for puncture wounds made by antlers. Of the 15 mule and white-tailed deer that were yearling males, seven had no antler scars. But of 12 bucks that were 2½ years of age and older, all had evidence of antler scars. Six bucks that were 2½-years-old had between seven and 31 wounds. Three bucks that were 3½ years of age had between 19 and 65 wounds. The oldest whitetail buck (6½ years) had 46 puncture wounds from fighting. The next oldest (5½ years) had 38 puncture wounds. Most scars were on the legs and the neck, but there were puncture wounds that entered the chest cavity, and apparently those animals survived and were later harvested by hunters (the source of the tanned hides used in the study was from hunters).

Geist noted that in field work on rutting mule deer he saw 24 visible combat injuries for 162 bucks that were over two years of age (15 percent incidence of wounding). Geist concluded that "the notion that fighting in cervids is a harmless ritual is not tenable."

That makes sense when you consider that antlers grow and develop all summer, and reach their yearly maximum size right before the rut. Then after the rut, the antlers drop off and the cycle begins again. This process is timed perfectly for the rut when competition between males reaches its peak. And as we have seen from the above stories and data, the fighting between bucks can get pretty serious at that time of the year. Earlier in the fall, after the velvet is shed, bucks push and shove in a ritualized manner, but come the rut, things can get nasty. Earlier in the fall you can see bucks travel together, groom each other, push and shove each other a bit. But once the does come into estrus, these "buddies" become competitors and fights do erupt.

Clearly, older bucks fight and hurt each other. Yet, deaths from the actual wounds inflicted upon other deer are not common. It would make no evolutionary sense for bucks to commonly kill each other. In another study Dr. Geist noted that antlers are shaped so as to hold and bind the heads of the two combatants together leading to "wrestling" rather than killing. Deer do not ram each other per se, they just push and shove, testing their strength one against the other. As we've seen from the above-mentioned data, they

(left) Unquestionably one of the rarest occurrences in the whitetail world is the observation of a pair of bucks entangled by their antlers, but with one of the combatants remaining alive, it could be considered phenomenal. On January 26, 1988, we discovered quite by accident another locked pair, again with only one survivor.

(below) Emaciated and extremely weak from hauling the dead combatant around for several days while fending off coyotes, this huge buck perished while an attempt was made to free him.

(opposite bottom) Bucks that die from antler-related injuries are often discovered in and around water. Our consensus on why this happens is the survivor attempts to avoid predators or assuage elevated body temperatures related to infection by soaking in the water.

do puncture each other in the body cavity, and there can be damage to the eyes during their fights. But, in general, these knock-down, drag-out fights do not usually lead to death, even though it may look that way. However, note that the rut, and fighting, does seriously reduce the health of these older bucks, making them more susceptible to death during bad winters.

Interestingly, we now know from scientific studies that dominant bucks in an area usually remain "on top" for only one year, and we also know that 3½ and 4½-year-old bucks probably do more mating than older bucks do. In fact, research suggests that the animals with the very biggest antlers (say 6½ years of age and older) may not always participate in the rut to the extent that younger, bigger bucks (say 3½) do. Dr. Val Geist noted that red stags that had the biggest antlers "were severely handicapped by their unwieldy antlers in fighting and tended to lose out to normally antlered males. This suggests that in freeliving populations, male deer with exceptionally large antlers may be non-breeders, and thus individuals of low fitness."

It is an interesting scenario because the bucks that fight during the rut need to heal during the winter, and we know that the bucks that die in harsh winters are often older bucks. Thus, there may be no real advantage for a buck to have huge antlers, and to rut. Huge antlers are one thing. But using them to fight during the rut can only lead to an animal heading into the winter in less than the best condition, even if that buck was the victor in such fights.

Others suggest that big antlers intimidate rivals to the point where they do not need to fight. They further suggest that females recognize the buck's superiority by the size of his body and antlers. Thus, this theory suggests that big-antlered bucks do have an advantage over bucks with lesser antlers. Maybe so. Perhaps the reality is that

Although antler wounds can prove fatal, most buck confrontations are actually bluffs. But when the combatants do engage in combat, it seldom lasts more than a minute or two.

even though whitetail bucks reach their maximum antler size when they reach the age of 5½ or 6½ years they may not be as physically fit as younger bucks. Since most does are mated by bucks that are 3½ and 4½ years of age, perhaps those bucks are more physically fit, even though their antlers may be a bit smaller than older bucks. Since bucks don't talk our language, and since observing and collecting data on such bucks is extremely difficult, we may never know the real answers here.

Many big bucks will fight other big bucks each year. We know that. What we do not know is what percentage of the heavy-duty fights lead to death. But when big bucks get locked together, unless found and freed by hunters or others, they will probably remain locked, till death do us part.

(right) Covered with antler puncture wounds, this buck perished only minutes after it was discovered.

SIZE MATTERS: SCORING AND AGING BUCKS ON THE HOOF

You've been practicing quality deer management on your hunt club property for three years. Club rules allow shooting does as well as bucks that score 125 inches or more and the rules are very clear. No mistakes are tolerated by your hunt club. It's the first day of the season and with anticipation high, you are up early and in the stand well before daylight. All the scouting and hard work are about to be rewarded because at first light, down the trail comes a good buck.

He is only an eight point, but the biggest buck you've seen in several years. As he steps into the shooting lane at twenty-two yards, you hesitate. He looks great, but will he meet the club's 125-inch mini-

mum? With seconds to decide, you pass the shot, not wanting to upset your club members.

With more and more states, hunting clubs, leases, and private landowners going to antler restrictions and increased doe harvests, making quick decisions on whether a buck is a shooter is a scenario that will be repeated often in the coming years.

(left) Scoring a buck on the hoof is extremely challenging simply because a mature buck will seldom remain stationary for very long.

(below) Seldom is the rack on a harvested buck larger than what you initially assumed. Many times that buck will have smaller antlers than you thought when the shot was taken. It's referred to as "ground shrinkage."

(above) This great Illinois buck scored 190 6/8 and was the top typical buck taken with the bow from 2006-2008. The hunter was Joel Eggers. Not many of us will get to see such a buck in our lifetime. No need to waste time field judging a rack of these proportions. (photo by Dave Samuel)

a genuine desire to fine tune their field-judging skills.

One method to improve field judging skills is to observe a lot of mature bucks. But how often does an individual entertain the view of a 160-class buck (based on the Boone and Crockett scoring system), or even a 150-class buck?

(below) We would venture to say that most hunters would be happy to see a buck scoring in the mid 130s during the hunting season.

(bottom) Estimating the dimensions of mounted deer is an efficient way to improve one's ability to score bucks on the hoof.

Even though we've bow-hunted many years, we still wrestle with the snap decision needed when judging whether a buck is a shooter or not. Once a doe or two are in the freezer, we focus on bigger bucks, but many hunters then use a self-imposed lower limit of 125 Boone and Crockett or Pope and Young points on the bucks they will attempt to harvest.

Estimating antler size on the hoof has become an integral part of both deer management and hunter satisfaction. Not long ago, the weight and point count of a buck sufficed when describing a successful hunt. Today, it's "what did it score and how old was the buck?"

The determination of antler score in the wild is challenging. Seldom will a mature buck remain stationary and in the right position long enough for a hunter to estimate its antler size. Sometimes the only view the hunter gets is that of a white tail as the animal bounds off. And shooting a buck that turns out to have a smaller rack than estimated can be downright discouraging. It's incredible how many inches of antler dissipate from the time of the shot to the time when the animal is recovered. It's called "ground shrinkage." Because estimating antler score adds another dimension to hunting while serving as another method of defining the entire experience, sportsmen have exercised

Not too often, and for most hunters, a 130-class buck is a relatively rare occurrence.

Possibly the most efficient method of improving antler scoring skills is to take advantage of what is most available—mounted deer heads.

Whenever a whitetail mount is observed, estimate it's inside spread, the number and length of points, the length of each main beam, and the average mass. Carry a small metal tape to verify your estimates. Before long, you will estimate the buck's gross score within an inch or two. More importantly, by confirming and adding up your measurements, you will learn just what attributes represent the greatest percentage of the rack's final score.

(right) Spread is an extremely attractive feature, but it represents only one measurement towards the final score.

(below) Follow up your estimates of a mounted head by actually measuring the animal. By doing so, you will not only improve your accuracy, but more importantly you will become more familiar with those measurements that contribute most to the final score

Spread

Some hunters place too much emphasis on antler spread. No question, the spread is a very attractive feature, but it represents only one measurement toward a rack's cumulative score. The comparison of the inside spread measurement and length of beams demonstrates this point.

For example, if a buck's rack exhibits an inside spread of 20 inches, a total of 20 inches is added to the final score. With 20-inch-long main beams, a total of 40 inches would be added to the final score for beams alone. With practice, one can become more familiar with the important components of the Boone and Crockett scoring system (see Chapter 13), and the antler measurements that count most. It's also important to note that the inside spread cannot exceed the length of the longest beam. In other words, a deer

can exhibit an inside spread of 30 inches and be super attractive but if its beams are only 23 inches long then only 23 inches of the spread is added to the accumulative score.

When a buck looks in your direction, make a quick judgment of spread. If the outside spread is two inches past each ear, it's a good spread. If the antlers are four inches or more past each ear, that buck has great spread. But official scoring uses the inside spread. Estimating inside spread is based on the space between ear tips when in the alert position. This measurement on mature bucks is around 18-19 inches in the North and 16 inches in the South. Thus,

(left) When a buck has antlers that go four inches beyond each ear, he has great spread. Few hunters would pass up this buck.

(below) This is a good, but not great, eight pointer. Note there are two points standing up (hence an eight pointer). Also note that the G2 is longer than the G3, and the inside beam skirts the ear tips, making him 16 inches wide.

Bowhunter Kevin Wilson from Alberta took this good buck in 2008. Though the ears are not quite fully extended in this photo, it appears that the inside spread is about two inches beyond each ear tip, making this a "good" buck. And check out the body size on this giant from the North. (photo by Kevin Wilson)

if the inside of the beams lies just outside the ears, the inside spread is 16-18 inches depending on where you are hunting. If the beam extends one inch past the ears, you're looking at a 18 to 20-inch inside spread. If the beam extends four inches past the ears you're looking at an inside spread of 24 to 26 inches. But remember, spread represents only one measurement towards total score, thus little time should be spent on this aspect. We also recommend that you should obtain some ear tip measurements from harvested bucks in your hunting camp to verify that distance as ear length varies by region and subspecies of deer.

Number of Points

Let's now look at the number of points. When you spot that buck, count the tines that stick up from one main beam, excluding the brow tines. If you see one main tine, he is probably a six point (one tine, one brow point, and the tip of the main beam on each antler). If you see two tines sticking up, then he probably

is an eight point. Three points up, it is a 10-pointer; and four points up, you're looking at a 12-pointer. Assuming the opposite antler is similar to the one being critiqued and both have a brow tine, the estimate should be close. High-scoring deer usually have at least three points up—ten points. However, exceptionally large eight-pointers can outscore 10-pointers. Point count is difficult if you run into a nontypical racked buck with points protruding everywhere, but when you get in this situation, you should be shooting, not counting.

(opposite left) Two tines up on one side, it's an eight pointer. Note it has a short G4 (look closely) on the right beam, but in order for it to be counted towards the final score, that tine must be at least one-inch long and taller than it is wide.

(above) Both of the bucks are broadside with three tines sticking up, making them 10 pointers. The G2 on the buck on the left is about the same length as its face (straight line down through the eye), making him a decent buck, but not great. For a bow-hunter, he is probably not a record-book buck.

(top right) With four tines standing up on each beam, this wide monarch is a potentially high-scoring 12 pointer.

(right) Nontypical points add character to a rack. A hunter seeing such a unique animal should be shooting, not counting.

Tine Length

Tine length contributes a lot to the final score, but determining tine length is difficult if you try to examine every tine. Since time is of the essence, just look at the overall tine length. This can be done by comparing the rack size to the face size. If the overall tine height is shorter than face height, it's a low quality buck. If the tine height is 1½ times the face height, it's a "good" buck. If the tine height is twice the size of the face, then that buck has excellent tine length. Ear length can also be utilized to estimate tine length. The length of a deer's ear is approximately eight inches. Thus, the ears represent a good reference when obtaining tine length. Sometimes a buck with more points will score less than a buck with fewer points. For instance, a 10-point deer with an average tine length of six inches would not score as well as an eight-point buck with 12-inch tines. Each antler point in excess of one inch is measured. Thus, tine length plays a significant role in the final score.

This buck is the third best typical buck entered into the Pope and Young records between 2006-08. It was taken by Barry Rose in Wisconsin and scored 187 2/8. Note the G2 tine length is about twice the length of the face (straight line down through the eye). This is just one of the characteristics making this an exceptional buck. However, no quick judgment would be needed to decide whether to shoot at this buck. You'd shoot as soon as a good shot presented itself. (Photo by Dave Samuel)

This may only be an eight point buck, but with mass and extremely tall tines complimented by a wide spread it gross-scored 160 inches. This guy was one of the most impressive bucks my (BZ) wife Jan ever shot and one of the most impressive eight pointers I have ever seen.

Main Beam Length

Now let's go to a very critical measurement that can best be made when the buck is broadside presenting a side view: main beam length. This can be done in seconds if you just focus on the tip of the main beam relative to the nose of the buck. Beams that curve backward initially, and then extend around and in front of the nose are approximately 25 inches in length. Note, often the main beam is not horizontal, so you must mentally lower the beam tip until it is horizontal.

If the tip of the main beam only extends to the eye, then it is an average quality buck. If it extends to the white muzzle around the nose, then it is a "good" main beam length. If it extends to the tip of the nose or beyond, then beam length is "excellent."

There is one other thing to consider. Often the main beams curve inward at the

(left) With wide sweeping beams extending beyond its nose, this record-book buck has 28-inch beams that add 56 inches to its total score.

tip. Again, just mentally straighten the main beam and then evaluate whether the tip reaches the white muzzle or the nose or beyond (see photo below). Estimating beam length can be difficult at first, but by practicing on mounted deer, one can become quite efficient at it. Again obtaining the average length of beam from deer harvested on the area you hunt can help distinguish between exceptionally long versus short beams.

(right) The main beams on most bucks that are eight points curve in at the tip. To decide whether the main beams will reach the nose or not, mentally straighten out the beam. Though this buck is not the widest spread buck in the world, he appears to have good tine length. When he sheds the velvet, he will probably have fairly good mass and will score fairly good for a bow kill.

(opposite bottom left) If the tip of the main beam only extends to the eye, then the buck has relatively short beams, but this guy has lots of mass, which adds much to its uniqueness and score.

(opposite bottom right) This buck has good main beams because the tip of the antler reaches the nose then curves upward, adding several inches to overall beam length.

(below) When this buck sheds his velvet, the main beam will be beyond the nose when seen from the side. This is one indication of an excellent buck.

Mass

Finally we come to mass. This is a rather subtle measurement, but a heavy-massed buck can make up for short tines or narrow spread. If the beam base is less than one-half as big as the ear base, the buck has little mass. If the beam base is three-fourths the size of the ear base, he has good mass. And if the antler base equals the ear base, this buck has great mass. Antler circumference measurements are recorded from four positions on each beam, thus a total of eight measurements are collected (see Chapter 13). A hunter should be able to differentiate between extremely light and heavy antlers. Extremely heavy beams that retain their mass throughout the beam add substantially to final score. Remember, a total of eight circumference measurements are calibrated, and it doesn't take long to accumulate a substantial amount of points.

Knowledge of the average mass produced by mature deer in your region is key to successfully estimating circumference measurements. This information helps differentiate between light and above average weight beams.

(above) The Alberta buck that shed these antlers had to have been huge. The mass on this buck is exceptional. Note this shed hunter's fingers barely fit around the antlers. These sheds were found by friends at Wizard Lake Outfitters. This Boone and Crockett whitetail is still out running around. (photo by Gunther Tondeleir)

(right) The most efficient method of acquiring the skill to score deer on the hoof is to measure all the bucks harvested on your hunting area. Sportsmen performing this activity are at least aware of what an average buck for their area scores and they will begin to recognize those bucks that exhibit above-average antlers.

Adding It Up

Remember, in the field you may have only seconds to judge antler quality, so how do we combine these five assessments into a quickly estimated field score? First, the buck must be at least an eight point to be a quality buck. If three of the four remaining assessments are "good," it's a shooter. In fact, you really only need to quickly assess beam length, spread, and tine length, because if a buck has all these, then it usually has good mass.

In short, if he has eight or more points, has a main beam that extends to the nose, has tines 1½ to 2 times

(top) With 10 tall tines, great spread, and long beams, little time should be spent estimating mass, particularly on this amazing buck.

(right) Antlers on a buck tend to look bigger as they walk away from you. If he wasn't big enough facing you, then he won't be as he walks away.

(bottom) Note the difference in size of G2s and G3s.

the height of the face, then it's a shooter most of the time. If he is good in only two of the four measurements, then the buck is probably in the 120-inch range.

Take that same buck and assume that he scores "good" in all four assessments. When that is the case, add ten inches. If that same buck is "excellent" in mass or tine length, then add another ten inches.

Antler coloration can make field judging score a bit more difficult. Dark-colored racks particularly when wet tend to appear massive, whereas light-colored antlers appear smaller, particularly in direct sunlight. Also, position of the animal can present estimation problems. Remember that antlers appear much bigger on a buck walking away from you, so a good rule of thumb is if you passed on a shot when the buck faced you, let it walk.

Over the past 33 years, we have looked over a large number of trophy bucks, and by doing so have learned that a rack that appears big does not always score high. There are some attributes that separate exceptional from average-sized racks.

If, for instance, the buck you are judging exhibits huge dimensions in appearance, critique the G2 tine, which is the first tine above the brow tine. If it is equivalent in length to the next tine (G3), and all tines are exceptionally long,

(below) Even though this buck has an average spread and mass, his tines are extremely tall and the G2s are as tall as its G3s, adding much to its final score of 191 inches.

you're looking at a high-scoring buck. I have yet to see a mature buck with G3s equal in length to the G2s that didn't score well (assuming all tines were long).

Whenever we see a buck, we immediately place it into a scoring category such as 120, 130, or 140 etc. Once placed in a category, we refine the score. For example, if a buck in the 130-inch category remains stationary long enough, then we work to refine my score and place it in the high or low 130s. If time permits, we will estimate its score as accurately as possible.

One technique I (BZ) employ when instructing students on scoring deer is a timed scoring test using 15 to 20 racks of various sizes hung on a fence 50 yards from the participants. The racks are placed in different positions, and observers utilizing binoculars are allowed 40 seconds to score each rack. When all racks are scored they are taken down and measured by the participants to verify their estimates. Not only is it beneficial to the students, it helps me polish my scoring ability as well. And judging a rack through a binocular lens is much closer to the real thing. In order to estimate antler size in the wild, quality binoculars are imperative. Purchase the best pair you can afford, and practice often.

Antler score is often skewed because of asymmetry. For example, if the side of the rack you are viewing appears large, there is no guarantee the opposing side

is identical. Thus if one beam, for instance, is 25 inches long, and the other is 23 inches, two inches will be subtracted from the final score. This difference, referred to as a "deduct," is accumulated from all matched measurements and subtracted from the gross score. The net score is what is registered into the record book because the Boone and Crockett scoring system is based on symmetry. In other words, a perfectly symmetrical 10-point buck could breach the required 170-inch mark and be accepted into the Boone and Crockett record book while a larger twelve-pointer grossing 190 inches might not be accepted simply because of all deductions caused by antler asymmetry. Asymmetry keeps a number of big bucks out of the record book. So, don't feel discouraged if your buck has a super gross score but less than an acceptable net score. A buck does not need to make the record book to be considered outstanding. The defining point of a trophy deer does not depend on score alone, but how it was hunted and, above all, that you like it.

Using Gross Score to Age Deer

Gross score can also be employed as an effective method for aging live deer. Dr. Charles DeYoung and his associates at Texas A and M University at Kingsville, found that the gross score was the best individual characteristic when it comes to estimating the age of deer on the hoof because it takes in all antler dimensions. By employing antler mass, spread, and tine length, along with neck and shoulder characteristics, DeYoung and his associates were able to estimate the age of marked deer with an amazing 89 percent accuracy.

Before ending this chapter, let's talk about the age that a buck reaches its maximum in antler size. Dr. Mickey Hellickson conducted research in Texas where they captured and collared hundreds of bucks over a 13-year period. Each year they attempted to recapture and score as many bucks as possible, and using this approach they learned that in South Texas, bucks reach they antler peak at 6½ years of age.

Interestingly, all but one of the various antler measurements did not reach their maximum until that

(top photos left to right)

This buck would immediately be placed in the low 120-inch category.

With G2s equivalent to the G3s, this buck would be placed into the higher 120-inch category.

This buck would be placed on the low end of the 130-inch category.

This buck, exhibiting a great spread, good beams, but short tines, would be placed in the 140-inch category.

With 10 tall tines, great spread, and above-average mass, this buck would be immediately placed into the 160-inch category.

(left) When you find a good collection of antler sets, hang them on a fence or building and practice scoring them. Keep a small tape with you to double check your estimates. Experience such as this will make you a better scorer in the field under hunting conditions.

(below) This buck I (BZ) shot in 2001 has it all. Wide heavy beams and 12 symmetrical tines, earning it a coveted spot in the Boone and Crockett record book.

same age. These included main beam length, basal circumference, etc. However, inside spread did not reach it's maximum until age 7½ years. And various body measurements such as weight and chest girth did not reach their maximum until 7½ years. The researchers suggest that the peak antler age of 6½ holds for Texas, but is probably earlier in other parts of the country. Our guess is that in states such as Iowa, Kansas, Illinois, etc., the antlers reach their peak at 5½ years.

Hellickson ran some statistical tests to find out which antler characteristic best ages bucks on the hoof. Their finding? Gross Boone and Crockett score is the single best measurement that predicts the age of the buck. The second best measurement for estimating age was basal circumference, but inside antler spread was also very good.

They also found something quite interesting. No one body characteristic was good for determining age after 2½ years, but from visual observations of known-aged bucks, Hellickson noted that stomach girth is still useful for aging bucks in the field. Mature bucks have stomachs that sag below the brisket. Hellickson suggests that you use gross antler score combined with stomach girth to give you the best estimate of a buck's age in the field. But the measurements that work for South Texas may not work for Ohio, or Missouri, or wherever. Wherever you hunt, you need to begin keeping mental data on bucks that you follow each year on camera or by sight, to determine the best field characteristics that allow you to determine age of the buck.

Deer hunters are achievers, and they continually raise their personal standards. Thus they place more demands on themselves in order to achieve their dream of taking that deer of a lifetime. The only problem is that big bucks are rare; actually they are aberrations of nature. Collecting a free-ranging super buck is like winning a million dollar lottery. It is rare, but possible. Therefore, to better your chances, you must be prepared to be able to identify that trophy before you take the shot. Practice your skills at scoring deer, maintain good hunting skills, and some day your number may come up and you may win the lottery—a Boone and Crockett whitetail!

WHAT IS A TROPHY?

It's a given that a trophy buck is whatever the hunter perceives. My first buck was a spike at age twelve, my first day gun hunting for deer. I promise you that for several years, that buck was an unbelievable "trophy" in my eyes and heart. The word "trophy" comes from Old French, trophee, from Latin, trophaeum, monument to victory. The dictionary defines trophy as "a lion's skin, deer's head, etc. displayed as evidence of hunting prowess," and "any memento." There are other definitions that are given in Webster's dictionary, but they relate to war.

For me, at age twelve that spike was a "trophy." However, as a hunter, as I

My (BZ) daughter Beth's buck will not make the record book, but it is a trophy in her mind. More importantly, she liked the animal and enjoyed the hunt, especially because her dad was there to help.

ing for those standing around while someone scores those antlers. We're not sure why we score antlers, but knowing the exact score is a way to compare one buck to another. Whether it is having the nicest yard in the neighborhood, or getting the highest grades in your high school class, or cooking the best tasting desserts, we are into competition. Having the animal scored, whether officially for the record book or unofficially

aged my goals changed. No matter. A trophy is whatever standard you set for yourself at a particular place and time. But various organizations have set minimum standards that a buck has to meet to qualify for their record book. Call them "trophies" if you will, or just call the bucks that meet those minimum standards "really nice animals." Regardless, thousands of hunters seek big bucks every year, and some that are successful enter them into a record book.

(above) The anticipation as to what that buck will score is fun for all ages of hunters in a hunting camp and it represents a measure of success relative to the camps management program.

(top right) Here college students assist me (BZ) scoring a huge nontypical. Measuring such a buck takes time and assistance.

(right) Antler size is often collected by sportsmen and managers alike as a yardstick measurement to determine the deer's response to the various management techniques employed. It also enhances one's ability to judge bucks on the hoof.

There is something about scoring antlers that interests hunters. They see a set of antlers and immediately take a guess at the score. "I wonder how big he is?" A common question. And if there are stickers or some nontypical points, that makes it all the more interest-

just to know how big that buck was, is something that many hunters like to do.

There are several national organizations that record bucks for their record books. They list the names and sizes of whitetail bucks that meet a certain minimum score for entry. But these books contain much more than a listing. In essence such books are history books as well as a biological record that provides reference points for measuring management success or failure. There are other points of reference that can be used to measure management policies, but antler size is one important measure.

The oldest scoring system is used by Boone and Crockett Club, The Pope and Young Club, and the National Muzzle Loading Rifle Association. Boone and Crockett and Pope and Young have the largest record books. Both have been keeping records for many years, and both have the most stringent requirements and training for their official scorers. While the Boone and Crockett Club, The Pope and Young Club, and the National Muzzle Loading Rifle Association utilize the same scoring system, there is a difference. The standards for entry into the Pope and Young Club record book are lower because they enter bucks taken with the bow.

These three clubs use the traditional system that puts bucks into the typical or nontypical categories. To enter a buck into the all-time Boone and Crockett record book, the minimum score for a typical buck is 170 inches, and 195 for a nontypical buck. In order to enter the awards book, which is updated every three years, the minimum score for a typical buck is 160 inches and 185 inches for a nontypical. Many bucks entered into Boone and Crockett are gun kills, but bow kills are also accepted. The minimum score for a typical buck taken with the bow and entered in the Pope and Young record book is 125 inches for typicals and 155 inches for nontypical bucks. The minimum for the Longhunter book is 130 inches for the typical category and 160 for nontypicals.

In addition, one can have his/her buck scored and entered into the Safari Club International record book or the Buckmasters record book.

Some nonhunters and a few hunters are happy to criticize all of these groups for creating their scoring methods and record books, believing that it creates a bad atmosphere for hunting by honoring trophy hunters. We discussed the erroneous beliefs concerning the trophy hunter in our 2008 book, *Whitetail Advantage*,

and won't reiterate that here. However, all of these groups with record books place a major emphasis on conservation and, via the books and other activities, they raise and spend hundreds of thousands of dollars every year on important conservation projects. Those funds are made available because hunters pay to have their quality animals honored by entering them in the respective record books. Those books help make hundreds of conservation and wildlife management projects a reality every year.

Gross vs. Net Score

One of the defining questions relative to scoring is whether to use the gross score or the net score. Boone and Crockett and Pope and Young use the net scores, while Safari Club International and Buckmasters use the gross score.

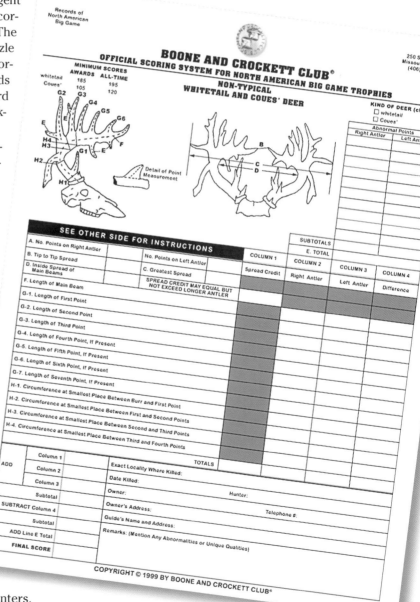

Official Boone and Crockett score sheet for nontypical entries. (with permission of the Boone and Crockett Club)

Our purpose here is not to take sides (though we, Bob and Dave, each have our preferred methods for scoring), but rather to present the methods used by each organization to honor large whitetail bucks.

There are arguments—good ones—for scoring methods that use the net score and those that use the gross score. For example, those supporting the use of the gross score say that it best represents the amount of antler that the buck actually grew on his head. One might counter that argument by pointing to bucks such as "cactus bucks" discussed in Chapter 10, and other nontypical bucks where antler growth was "more than what would normally form" due to injuries to the velvet as the antler grew. Regardless of which scoring strategy you prefer, the system used by Boone and Crockett and Pope and Young has the most tradition. They have used the net score for years and apparently want to adhere to tradition. In addition, changing the scoring system for Boone and Crockett and Pope and Young would make comparisons to all the bucks previously entered in prior years difficult.

Les Davenport, in an excellent article on "gross vs. net" in the September 2007 issue of *North American Whitetail* magazine, noted that most hunters simply categorize their bucks as "small, medium, big and monster." He then went on to state that this type of antler characterization is what stimulated the Boone and Crockett Club to create a standard scoring system.

That system adds up deductions and uses them to create a net score. That scoring system was started in 1932 and modified in 1950, with minimum standards for deer created in order for bucks to qualify for the Boone and Crockett record book. The evolution of this system is long and circuitous, but it essentially has a typical category that measures inside spread, beam length, tine length, and circumference measurements on both antlers, and deducts the differences. Then there is the nontypical category that takes the same measurements, but also adds in the lengths of abnormal points.

From our observations, most hunters prefer to shoot big, typical bucks, with eye appeal and symmetrical racks. However, there are some hunters that search for those nontypical antlered bucks. The more nontypical, the better.

Bottom line though, if given the choice of two bucks looking at them, one being nontypical, one typical, but the nontypical is bigger, most hunters will shoot the biggest buck. However, one must remember that the score of a buck's antlers is not the measure of whether a hunt is successful or not. The buck taken may not meet the standards of a particular record book, but it still may be a great buck. Think about that for a minute. If a gun-harvested, typical buck scores 170 1/8 inches, it qualifies for the Boone and Crockett record book, but if another buck scores 169 7/8 inches, that buck does not qualify. Is the one buck greater than the other? Is the hunter who took the second buck greatly despondent because the buck missed the book? If you answered "yes" to either of these questions, you may be hunting for the wrong reasons.

The official score of a buck is a reference point—one that allows historical comparisons, regional difference comparisons, and a set, solid number for any comparison.

Differences in Scoring Among the Organizations

We've noted above that Boone and Crockett, Pope and Young, and Longhunter (muzzleloading) use net scores. But Safari Club International and Buckmasters use gross scores. For the first three organization record books, you take the maximum inside spread of the main beams (this measurement cannot exceed the longest main beam in length). Then you also take the length of each main beam, the length of the first point (G1), second point (G2), third point (G3), the fourth point (G4) if present, and all points out to G7, if present. Then take the circumference at the smallest place between the burr and the first point, etc. (do for each point ending with circumference between the third and fourth points or half way between the third point and beam tip if the fourth point is missing). Finally, deduct the differences in each of these measurements from one antler to the other. Add up all measurements and deduct the differences and you have the net score. If there are nontypical points anywhere, and you are scoring the buck as a typical buck, then you deduct the length of the nontypical points. It can get a bit tricky determining what an abnormal point is, but such determinations must be made and deductions assessed.

This figure demonstrates where the inside spread is taken. It's important to note that C, the greatest outside spread and B, tip-to-tip spread, are for identification purposes and do not contribute to the final score. (with permission of the Boone and Crockett Club)

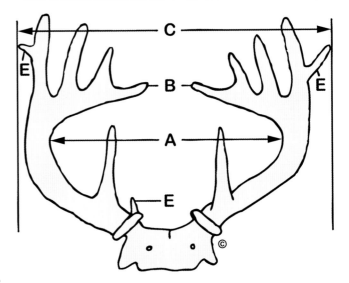

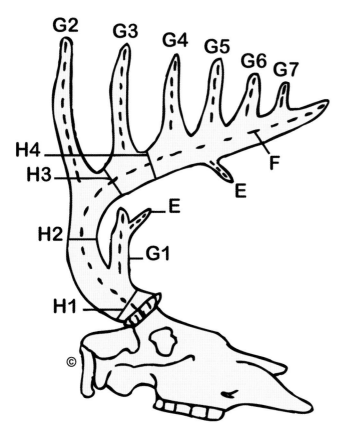

This side view demonstrates the location of the length of beam and, more importantly, where the measurement should be taken along with tine length and the four circumference measurements.

For nontypical bucks, one measures the inside spread, beam lengths, and circumferences as with typical bucks. One also calculates the deductions as done with typical racks. But you also then add the length of all abnormal points.

In order for a point to be counted, it must be longer than it is wide and one inch long. A steel tape can be used to designate where the point begins.

The Safari Club system is similar, but there are differences. Take the inside spread, the length of each beam, the length of each tine, and the circumference measurements as noted above. You do not add in deductions. The Buckmaster system is similar to Boone and Crockett to a degree, but there are significant differences. Here you take the length of each beam, the length of each tine, and the circumference between all points as noted above (but you are not limited to four circumference measurements). There are no spread measurements and no deductions.

Also note that since there is no inside spread measurement for Buckmasters, you can include bucks where the skull plate is broken or separated. In addition, their minimum scores for entry are lower than those for Boone and Crockett or Pope and Young, the reason being that no inside spread measurements count toward the score. For guns, the minimum score to enter a buck in the Buckmaster's book is 140, and for bow the minimum is 110. You can also enter "pick-ups" and shed antlers. Only one antler is measured for the "shed" category with a minimum score of 75 inches need for entry.

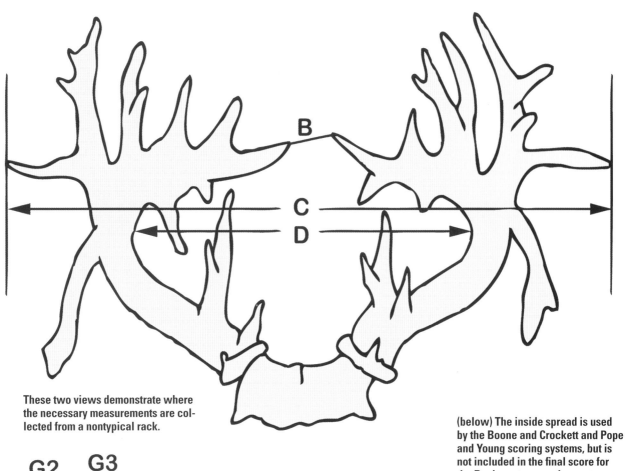

These two views demonstrate where the necessary measurements are collected from a nontypical rack.

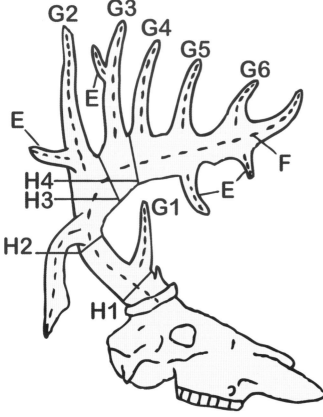

(below) The inside spread is used by the Boone and Crockett and Pope and Young scoring systems, but is not included in the final score for the Buckmasters scoring system.

High Fences and Fair Chase

Nothing gets under the radar these days. Every illegal hunting arrest is covered by the news. Even though a certain hunting practice might be legal, society will pass judgment on whether that practice is ethical. And ethical standards are changing. It wasn't all that long ago that dog hunting was not viewed in a negative light (see photo above). Now, even the use of beagles to hunt rabbits upsets lots of nonhunters. We support using beagles for rabbit hunting and wish more kids had the opportunity to grow up in a situation where

they could take their pet beagle and hunt rabbits. But the urban world doesn't see it that way.

Baiting is another topic that brings out differing opinions, even when legal. Drawing the line on baiting is an evolving process. We now hear a few people talking about hunting near acorns or corn fields as a form of baiting. We totally disagree with this perspective on "baiting," but

Dog hunting, once a popular sport in various parts of the South, has been shut down in many areas, yet dogs like my (BZ) Catahoula Rowdy are used (by permission) to track wounded deer.

the urban world doesn't always see it that way. Time marches on.

Most organizations that enter harvested whitetail bucks into their record books have some rules that they implement that set standards for entry. One is in regards to the use of high fences and hunting behind high fences. While the Boone and Crockett Club and The Pope and Young Club do not allow any animals taken behind a high fence to be entered in their record books, Safari Club International and Buckmasters do allow it.

Whether a club has a ruling against or in favor of high fences, they all have some ethics standards that must be met for entry. For example The Pope and Young Club mandates that you sign a "fair chase affida-vit" that defines fair chase as not taking an animal:

1. that is helpless in a trap, deep snow or water, or on ice.

2. from any power vehicle or power boat.

3. while inside escape-proof fenced enclosures.

4. by "jacklighting" or shining at night.

5. by the use of any tranquilizers or poisons.

6. by the use of any power vehicles or power boat for herding or driving animals, including use of aircraft to land alongside or to communicate with or direct a hunter on the ground.

7. by the use of electronic devices for attracting, locating, or pursuing game, or guiding the hunter to such game, or by the use of a bow or arrow to which any electronic device is attached.

Boone and Crockett does not allow a rangefinder within the scope of the gun. They also do not allow the use of any electronic callers or any animal taken where a cell phone or walkie talkie was used.

Big deer are cherished by all hunters. Whether they enter a record book or not is irrelevant because what such bucks actually represent most is a grand memory.

Conclusions

The world is changing, and the world of deer hunting is as well. Today it is relatively common for guides to have minimum standards for bucks they will allow a client to harvest. Make a mistake and shoot a buck that doesn't meet the minimum standards and you pay a fine. The guides work hard to manage their lands to get mature bucks for their clients and shooting younger bucks negatively impacts management goals. Thus, they charge a fine when young smaller bucks are harvested. Years ago, you never heard of a guide that had a minimum buck size that they'd allow their hunters to take. A sign of the deer hunting times.

Fair chase is also becoming critical relative to the hunting of "trophies." More and more we see the "fair chase" concept being promoted by hunting organizations, television hunting shows, and individuals. But one standard does not apply to all states. For example, you can use a crossbow in one state during the regular bow season, but not in some others. You can bait in some states, but not in others. As one author recently pointed out, "the concept (fair chase) was not created as a test to divide ethical hunters."

Individual hunters have their own set of values that they live by, whether hunting or doing other things in life. The taking of a large buck brings with it some responsibility, not only to the animal, but to other hunters and to society in general. It is also an individual's decision whether to call any buck taken a "trophy." One standard definitely doesn't fit all. But if you want your buck to be officially recognized, then you can find an organization that sets that standard, and you can have that buck entered for posterity.

Regardless what a deer scores, it represents a memorable experience. This was obviously the case when Ashley Strickland from Huntsville, Alabama, arrowed this P&Y buck with her recurve bow during the Kansas 2008 hunting season. Truly a hard-earned and well deserved trophy. (Photo photo by Warren Strickland)

WHERE DO THE BIG BOYS LIVE?

Get a group of traveled deer hunters together to discuss where to go for the biggest bucks, and the debate is on. It's easy to make educated "guesses" on which states hold more big bucks, but backing it up with real data is another issue entirely.

We know that big bucks are the result of three factors: age, nutrition, and genetics. For many hunters living east of the Mississippi River, the greatest limiting factor—the one that prevents bucks from reaching their full potential—is age. Though things are changing, in some states over 80 percent of all harvestable, legal, bucks are taken every year. This means that few bucks reach older age categories. You can't kill big bucks if they aren't there.

Pennsylvania once harvested as many as 90 percent of all legal bucks every year. But in 2002, they went to an antler restriction and hunters there are now

(below) Big antlers are a byproduct of age, nutrition, and genetics.

(right) A quality hunting experience means more than a kill, and unless young bucks are allowed to walk, an image of dragging a nice buck out of the forest remains only that—an image.

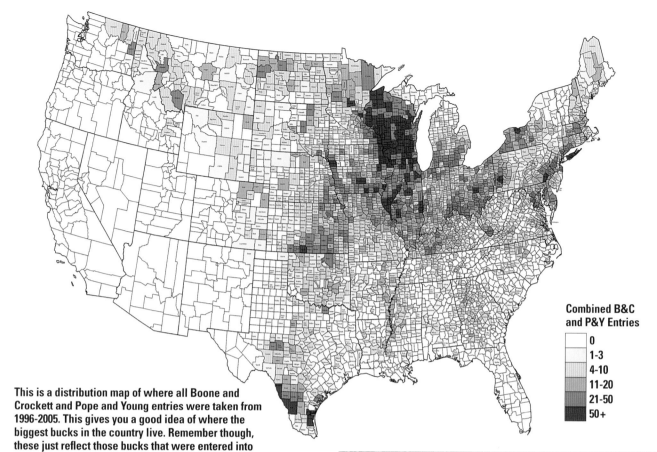

This is a distribution map of where all Boone and Crockett and Pope and Young entries were taken from 1996-2005. This gives you a good idea of where the biggest bucks in the country live. Remember though, these just reflect those bucks that were entered into the respective record books. (Compliments of the Quality Deer Management Association)

Combined B&C and P&Y Entries

	0
	1-3
	4-10
	11-20
	21-50
	50+

With the combination of a nutritionally diverse habitat and the ability to reach maturity, bucks anywhere are capable of demonstrating their desirable genetic qualities.

seeing and harvesting bigger bucks than ever. Other states are also making such changes.

The two main depositories of record bucks are the Boone and Crockett (guns) and Pope and Young (bows) record listings. However, a simple count of states where the record-book bucks were harvested has some biases and problems. First, such listings only record bucks that hunters decided to enter. Do all hunters from all states enter their animals at the same rate? If a higher percentage of hunters from one state actually enter their record-book bucks, then that would penalize other states where a lower percentage of hunters enter their kills. But, we have no data to prove that this happens, so we'll assume that the same percentage of hunters from all states enter their eligible bucks.

Second, the number of record-book bucks harvested in a state or province is obviously related to the number of big bucks that live there. That's an obvious given. But the harvest is also related to hunting pressure and the number of hunters there. Some super states, an example being Kansas, have a good percentage of big bucks, but comparatively fewer listed in the record books than one might expect simply because they don't have as many hunters. A prime example of a state that is at the top of the list for record bucks harvested is Wisconsin. Now Wisconsin is a great state for big bucks, but it also has a huge number of deer hunters compared to other states. In 2006 there were around 639,000 resident big game hunters 16 years of age and older in Wisconsin and only 142,000 resident big game hunters in Kansas. Those numbers of Wisconsin hunters definitely impact the number of record-book bucks harvested there. So, numbers of big bucks harvested per state, listed alone, does not give you an accurate comparative estimate of where big bucks are found. But it is part of the puzzle.

Our good friend (and outstanding deer researcher working for the King Ranch in Texas), Dr. Mickey Hellickson, published an interesting article in the September 1996 issue of *Deer and Deer Hunting* magazine. In that article ("Where Do Boone and Crockett Bucks Come From?") he tabulated all typical bucks scoring over 170 inches and all nontypicals scoring over 195 inches from the Boone and Crockett records. If you look at his top ten states (see column 1 in Table 1) for all bucks entered in the Boone and Crockett's records from 1830 through 1993, the top state was Minnesota. Then the rest of that list shows the importance of the Midwest farming states, and Texas and Montana are also in there. However, if you move to the same list from 1991-1993 (Table 1, column 2), some things have changed. Illinois, Kansas and Missouri all move up on the list, while Minnesota, Texas, and Wisconsin, move down the list. Montana drops out of the top ten and Indiana sneaks in.

Table 1. First column, top ten states for gun-harvested Boone and Crockett bucks entered from 1930-1993. Second column, top ten states for 1991-1993. Third column, top ten states and provinces for gun-harvested Boone and Crockett bucks, 2005-2007.

RANK	1930-1993		1991-1993		2005-2007 (rank only)
1	Minnesota	420	Illinois	81	Wisconsin
2	Iowa	317	Iowa	56	Illinois
3	Wisconsin	272	Minnesota	42	Kentucky
4	Illinois	224	Kansas	29	Saskatchewan
5	Texas	203	Missouri	29	Indiana
6	Kansas	128	Texas	28	Iowa
7	Missouri	119	Wisconsin	28	Minnesota
8	Ohio	109	Ohio	24	Ohio
9	Kentucky	97	Kentucky	18	Missouri
10	Montana	78	Indiana	15	Kansas

When it comes to big deer, Iowa ranks with the best and that is where Steve Binkley arrowed this 242 inch bruiser. It ranked #1 during the 2006-2008 period. (Photo by Dave Samuel)

deer at all in Illinois and Iowa. Then why are those states so high on the 1830-1993 lists? Because almost half the bucks entered for that period were taken from 1984-1993. In other words, it appears that once the population increased substantially in those states the number of big bucks also increased due to great soils, great feed, and lower hunting pressure (that allowed bucks to achieve some age).

So what changed in the early 1990s? We have no way of knowing, but Hellickson points out several factors that can influence the number of record-book bucks harvested in a state. First, remember that prior to the 1950s there just were not that many deer in the southern part of Minnesota and Wisconsin, and few

Relative to habitat, Hellickson pointed out that as acreage of crops increased, so did the size of bucks in the harvest. Then throw in acreage of land entered into the Conservation Reserve Program (CRP lands) and that helped too. Finally, Dr. Hellickson noted that the early 1990s were about the time when soybean production took off in the Midwest. This also led to bigger bucks. So the formula for growth of big whitetail bucks at that time (and today) seems to point to agriculture versus forests.

Corey Neil from Mississippi found this three-point shed antler in Canada. It scored 70 3/8 inches. With an average spread and the other side matching it would score 160 inches making it the largest six-point in the record book. Canada's top end is unreal! (Photo by Dave Samuel)

More agriculture and less forested land lead to bigger bucks. Better soils, especially along major rivers, leads to higher agricultural production, and this also leads to bigger bucks. High agriculture production with mast producing trees along those river bottoms is a recipe for big bucks.

All of those factors would help to explain why western Wisconsin, eastern Iowa, western Illinois, western Iowa, eastern Kansas, northeastern Missouri, southern Illinois, southern Indiana, western Kentucky, and southern Ohio are hot areas for big bucks.

Now let's move to 2005-2007 and see if there are any significant changes. We went through the 2005 Pope and Young Club record book and checked the states listed for the top 100 typicals and nontypicals taken with the bow (see Table 2). The "big 3" for typicals and nontypicals lists were Illinois, Iowa, and Kansas. These states have healthy habitats, bucks that survive to an older age, good genetics, great food, some major rivers (and associated river bottoms), and fairly good sex ratios of does to bucks.

If you compare this bow list to the top ten gun-harvested record book states in column 3 in Table 1, it gets a bit interesting. Remember though, that Table 2 is not a total count of Pope and Young bucks, just a count of the top 100 typicals and top 100 nontypical buck states. Anyway, note from column 3 in Table 1 that Saskatchewan ranked fourth for the number of record-book bucks taken with a gun from 2005-2007, but had only one typical taken with the bow up to

Table 2. Pope and Young Club 2005 bow record book listings and the 2006-2008 listings for the top ten states as measured by counting the top 100 typical and top 100 nontypical whitetail bucks.

2005 TYPICALS		2005 NONTYPICALS		2006-2008 TYPICALS		2006-2008 NONTYPICALS	
State	Number	State	Number	State	Number	State	Number
Illinois	25	Kansas	24	Illinois	22	Illinois	25
Iowa	22	Illinois	23	Wisconsin	14	Kansas	16
Kansas	19	Iowa	19	Kansas	12	Iowa	11
Ohio	7	Wisconsin	6	Iowa	8	Wisconsin	10
Minnesota	6	Minnesota	4	Indiana	8	Indiana	6
Wisconsin	5	Ohio	3	Missouri	7	Ohio	5
Indiana	2	Alberta, Oklahoma	2	Ohio	6	Minnesota	5
Nebraska	2	Nebraska, Indiana Missouri		Minnesota	4	Texas	4
Several others	1			Maryland	3	Kentucky	3
				Alberta	3	Several others	2

from 2006-2008 with the bow. Our guess is that the cold weather found in Saskatchewan in the rut dissuades bowhunters from going there. However, that is changing with the advent of ground blinds and heaters. In addition, Saskatchewan guides are learning how to place tree stands and ground blinds in the early part of the season when temperatures are more conducive to bowhunting. Expect to see more bowhunters taking bigger bucks in Saskatchewan in coming years.

Though numbers are not shown, another big difference is the large number of record-book bucks taken with the rifle from 2005-2007 in Wisconsin, Kentucky, and Indiana (column 3, Table 1). These states also look strong for recent listings of bow kills from 2006-2008 (Table 2). Wisconsin and Indiana are in the top five and Missouri, Ohio, and Minnesota are also doing well. Alberta is now in the top 10 with the bow. This probably reflects that more and more bowhunters are going there to hunt big deer. Alberta has them, and Kentucky is sneaking in there. Kentucky is producing more bigger bucks than ever before. The up-and-comers for this group of states would be Indiana, Missouri, and Kentucky. Iowa, Kansas, and Wisconsin will always be up there. Illinois should be as well, but their new (2009) two-buck rule now puts that state in jeopardy. Only time will tell how much of a negative impact this will have on the age structure of their buck harvest. But it can't be a positive.

Now compare which states were on top for bowhunters in 2005 to the overall best states for bowhunting record-book bucks from 1961 thru 2008. Table 3 shows the top 10 states for typical and nontypical bucks taken with the bow from 1961-2008 (Bowhunting Records of North American Whitetail Deer, third edition. This great record book gives you the top list by state and province and a ton of other interesting deer data. You can buy it at www.pope-young.org).

Wisconsin is a proven big buck state. But remember there is a bias here. They have lots of hunters. Still,

2005 (you can't see that in Table 2, but Saskatchewan was one of the states and provinces that had one buck in the top 100). Again, note that Saskatchewan had only one from the top 100

Kevin Radke took this awesome 239 4/8 inch buck in Illinois, demonstrating just how big those Illinois deer can get. (Photo by Dave Samuel)

Table 3. A list of the top 10 states for bow-killed bucks tabulated from the top 100 typicals and non-typicals from 1961-2008.

RANK	Typical Whitetails STATE OR PROVINCE	NUMBER OF ENTRIES	RANK	Nontypical Whitetails STATE OR PROVINCE	NUMBER OF ENTRIES
1	Wisconsin	8037	1	Illinois	643
2	Illinois	3279	2	Wisconsin	421
3	Iowa	3425	3	Iowa	407
4	Ohio	2594	4	Kansas	300
5	Minnesota	2124	5	Ohio	207
6	Kansas	1986	6	Minnesota	153
7	Indiana	1788	7	Missouri	144
8	Missouri	1547	8	Indiana	134
9	Michigan	1379	9	Texas	80
10	Texas	1350	10	Kentucky	71

a great place to hunt big bucks. And Wisconsin will continue to harvest lots of big bucks, one reason being that they harvest a substantial number of does and this really sustains healthy habitat. But the three states that should increase the most both in total numbers of record-book bucks and in the top 100 record-book bucks over the next ten years are Kentucky, Indiana, and Missouri. Since Indiana went to a one buck limit, they've seen an improvement. Except for some management areas, Kentucky also has a one buck limit, and that includes the harvest of a button buck. Missouri experimented with an antler restriction in some counties for the past four years and is expanding that for 2009 (see Chapter 20). That will improve the big buck potential by a huge amount. Missouri may well be the big sleeper in all of this. Watch for jumps there and in Kentucky and Indiana with bow and gun. And don't forget Oklahoma and Louisiana. They aren't on any top 10 lists as yet, but more and more hunters are headed to these states because more landowners are managing habitat (food plots, etc.) for good bucks.

One more point. Note that Illinois, Iowa, and Kansas have the lowest number of resident big game hunters for 2006 (see Table 4), yet they are in the top ten for the number of Boone and Crockett bucks taken from

Enhanced nutritionally by a variety of food plots, bigger deer will continue to show up in the harvest across the country.

2005-2007 (see column three, Table 1). Lower number of hunters and high numbers of big bucks. That tells you something.

In the latest Pope and Young Club Whitetail record book, they list the top 10 individual typical and nontypical bucks. The top 10 typicals came from Illinois (2), Iowa (2), Minnesota (2), Ohio (2), Saskatchewan (1), and Alberta (1). The top 10 nontypical bucks came from Kansas (4), Illinois (2), Iowa (1), Ohio (1), Nebraska (1), and Missouri (1).

Joel Helmer, in the Spring 2002 issue of *Fair Chase*, published by the Boone and Crockett Club, wrote a very interesting article on a geographic analysis of big

Table 4. The number of resident big game hunters, 16 years old and older, 2006.

Resident Big Game Hunters		# Big Game Days of Hunting
Wisconsin	639,000	7,950
Missouri	502,000	6,973
Ohio	432,000	2,201
Kentucky	242,000	3,832
Indiana	233,000	3,469
Illinois	216,000	2,728
Iowa	275,000	2,333
Kansas	142,000	1,239

bucks. To micro-tune the above state and province lists, he took it down to counties. The top six states with the most Boone and Crockett bucks harvested per county from 1892 to 2001 were Iowa (17 counties), Illinois (11), Wisconsin (6), Kentucky (4), Minnesota (4), and Texas (4). He also noted that the states with more big bucks harvested tend to have lower deer densities, shorter gun seasons, and low buck bag limits.

He also noted a huge relationship between big buck entries from counties that have large rivers flowing through them, especially in farm country.

As we stated at the outset, whether a state harvests a number of record-book bucks depends on a number of factors. Things have been happening of late to help that situation. For example, there is a trend in whitetail states to go to a one buck limit, and that definitely puts age on bucks. There is also a nationwide trend to harvest more does. That improves the health of the deer and the habitat, and the result will be bigger bucks. There is a trend to implement point restrictions and also quality deer management practices. Those will help the deer too.

We are seeing more landowners managing both habitat and harvest for bigger, healthier deer. This means that sleeper states such as Kentucky, Indiana, Missouri, and Oklahoma will continue to climb in the ranks with bigger harvests of great bucks.

Add all this up and you soon discover that relative to bigger bucks, the "good ol' days" are happening right now. Study the data and get out there and enjoy the fun.

(left) Limiting the buck harvest to only one buck per hunter per season will allow additional bucks the opportunity to enter the older, larger antler-producing age classes.

(below) Removing does to balance deer populations not only benefits the deer herd, but more importantly the habitat upon which deer depend.

COUNTING YOUR BUCKS: SURVEY TECHNIQUES

The quiescence of South Texas is interrupted each fall by the incessant drone of helicopters. The solid "whop" of the extended blades slicing the cool air can be distinctly heard as these hover craft crisscross the vast landscape like dragonflies over a stock tank. The occupants are wildlife biologists searching the low-lying brush for whitetail deer. Their objective is to obtain a deer population estimate upon which harvest recommendations are based.

Nowhere in the country are deer censused with such detail as in Texas. Since a lot of Texas deer hunting and management occurs on private land, much time, energy, and money is spent on getting good counts of the deer on a piece of property.

For years biologists employing the helicopter as a means of censusing deer were confident of counting a high percentage, if not all the deer, on the South Texas plains. However, even in this sparsely vegetated habitat, many deer escape from such efforts. Censusing a wild population, particularly deer, is extremely difficult, requiring biologists to acquire additional population information to supplement that obtained via aircraft.

A variety of techniques are used, and the information of each is often consolidated in order to come up with a reliable

(left) The helicopter is a popular deer survey tool in low-lying brush areas where ground visibility is limited.

(below) For years South Texas biologists assumed they were observing a high percentage of deer from a helicopter, but data now suggest that 40 percent of the population could go unobserved.

*Excerpted in part from the "Know Whitetails" column, May 2009 *Whitetail Journal*.

Counting Your Bucks: Survey Techniques | **129**

population estimate.

To conduct a deer survey, a variety of factors, including weather, habitat type, physical land features, etc., must be considered. For instance, a helicopter is an efficient survey tool in low-growing brush, but in a hardwood forest it is inadequate unless conducted following leaf fall. Even post leaf fall, tall trees prohibit aircraft from flying low enough to force deer to move and become more visible to the observers.

Deer herds are actually surveyed, not censused. A census is a complete count of animals over a specified area at a specified time. (Getting a total count on deer anywhere is difficult if not impossible. In fact, as we have discovered in this country, getting a total count of people in a city is difficult if not impossible). A survey on the other hand is a count of animals observable at the particular time, with the realization that animals, sometimes a substantial number, are not observed. To compensate for missed animals, surveys are often replicated in an attempt to come up with the best population estimate.

For example, when surveying deer with a spotlight,

results on a given night are dependent on variables such as moon phase and weather conditions, which directly impact deer activity. The time chosen may simply be a night when few deer are up and moving. Thus the deer population is underestimated. Setting a harvest quota based on a single night's survey would obviously not be as accurate as one based on results obtained over three or more nights with the observations averaged.

Techniques employed to survey deer populations include pellet group counts, walking predetermined census lines, track counts, spotlight counts, helicopter surveys, and infrared triggered camera surveys. All have their advantages, but managers realize that there is more

(top) Amazingly, some of the older bucks will remain cement-still until the craft passes it by; some will actually look up. Experienced observers are cognizant of this fact and do not depend on deer running from the craft. These guys literally search the brush floor, hoping to catch a glimpse of these reticent animals.

(above) Every time I (BZ) observe a buck on an aerial survey I place it into an age class category, and if I have time, I will estimate its gross Boone and Crockett score.

to a deer survey than simply counting deer to determine a population estimate.

Survey by Helicopter

The helicopter, for example, affords excellent visibility and the opportunity to observe a substantial number of deer in the semi-open Southwest. The paramount advantage of the helicopter survey is that a high percentage, 60 to 80 percent, of the entire deer population can be observed over a short period of time. The fact that 20 to 40 percent of the population is unobserved can be statistically adjusted in order to estimate population parameters.

Additional information is collected that will fortify previous management decisions or calls for adjustments in upcoming recommendations. One very important deer management objective is to get a balanced sex ratio. Thus, one of the most precise pieces of information gathered from this aerial use of helicopters is the sex ratio of the deer herd. Another piece of information needed is the percent survival of fawns, a vital part of recruitment dictating the planned harvest. Also extremely important is the fact that using a helicopter affords the trained eye a chance to determine

(left) This outstanding buck will breach the 160-inch benchmark, which on open range makes him a great trophy buck.

(bottom left) A variety of exotic wildlife can be observed from a helicopter on South Texas ranches, and all of them are recorded because they impact the habitat and, thus, the quality of whitetails on it. Exotics such as this nilgai are commonly found on South Texas ranches.

(below) Numbers of the whitetails' top predator, the coyote, are collected to determine when and if some control is needed.

the antler quality and age class structure for bucks.

While conducting aerial surveys, bucks are classified into five categories: spikes, yearling bucks, middle age bucks (three to four years of age), mature bucks (five plus), and a separate category of trophy deer which includes bucks exhibiting antlers in excess of desirable or expected gross Boone and Crockett score for the area, which in most places is 160 inches. Acquiring this information, the manager has an estimate of male age class structure plus the percentage of males developing rack size expected within the region.

Although a unique tool for the wildlife manager, the helicopter is not a necessity. It is an expensive tool that can be cost prohibitive. That's why it is important to gather as much information as possible while employing it. On our work in Texas we take observations of quail coveys, javelinas, feral hogs, bobcats, coyotes, exotic animals, even cattle. By doing so, predator control, if warranted, can be implemented along with adjusting domestic and exotic stocking rates, all of which play a critical role in wildlife management.

Other Survey Tools

The universal deer population survey tool is the spotlight. Its principal advantage is cost—it is affordable. All that is needed is some mode of transportation and three individuals—a driver and one person on each side of the vehicle handling the spotlights. While on a predetermined route, observers estimate the visibility range on each side of the vehicle at each tenth of a mile. The length of the route, in feet multiplied by the sum of all visibility distances, yields the amount of land viewed in square feet, which is then divided by 43,500 square

Although deer are quite visible from above, the thick vegetation often renders the conventional spotlight surveys ineffective.

feet, yielding the amount of land surveyed in acres. The principal disadvantage of a spotlight count is its dependency on deer behavior. Sometimes deer are up and moving, other times they are not. Thus, surveys must be repeated three to five nights in a row to obtain an adequate population estimate.

Quite possibly the most efficient way for sportsmen to acquire pertinent information on their particular deer herds is to employ what we refer to as windshield biology—incidental sightings. This technique is attractive because it is inexpensive, anyone can do it, and it can be conducted while the observer is driving around the property, even while they hunt.

To collect incidental sighting data, all that is required is a pad and pen. Each and every time a deer or group of deer is sighted, the number, sex, estimated age, as well as antler score in inches, if male, is recorded. With 10 to 15 deer hunters recording deer observations, it doesn't take long before a substantial amount of information is accumulated. Collecting information like this is an efficient way to obtain sex ratio, fawn survival, age class structure, as well as antler quality.

Incidental sightings can be conducted before the season during one's scouting trips or during the hunting season. Although it is not the ultimate population estimating tool, it lends itself to observing trends in population changes when compared annually. It also

affords supplemental information to support other survey techniques employed.

The development of infrared sensors that trigger cameras has afforded managers an additional way to estimate deer populations. This rather new technology was first reported by Harry Jacobson and his colleagues on a densely wooded 10,000-acre area in South Mississippi. By staging infrared triggered cameras over bait, the researchers found that in a period as short as ten days, they photographed 97 percent of the bucks and 72 percent of the does previously marked on the area.

The infrared cameras represent a unique opportunity to estimate deer populations as well as study deer behavior. With this technology, biologists, managers, and sportsmen will be able to enter the secret world of the whitetail and learn things that were a mystery up until now.

The principal advantage of this technology is that anyone can use it, it is inexpensive, and it is not overly time consuming. Since its inception, a variety of cameras at affordable prices have entered the market and,

(left) These two bucks were filmed on a 3.6-acre parcel owned by a friend of mine in Florida. He did not know he had a single deer on the property. Can you imagine his excitement when these guys showed up on film?

(below) Patterning certain bucks is now possible with trail cam photos, especially if they are as unique as this easily recognizable double beamed buck. (Photo by Gene Wensel)

like computers, they will become more efficient and less expensive in the future.

According to Jacobson, a complete census requires at least one camera station per 160 acres. By deploying cameras at sites frequented by deer such as food plots, feeders, etc., and making the site more attractive by displacing an attractant like corn, a high percentage of deer can be photographed. Obviously, the larger the area, the more cameras required, but there are ways to get around this obstacle.

For example, if you are attempting to estimate the deer population on a 2,000-acre area using five cameras (one per 200 ac.), simply obtain an aerial survey map of the area and grid the areas into 200-acre blocks. Select and bait ten numbered sites (one per block). Set cameras up at sites one through five for 10 days, then rotate them to blocks six through ten for another 10-day period. Be sure to have some sort of site identification number present in the photograph for reference. Once pictures are developed, each one must be scrutinized to identify individuals. This may be difficult at first, particularly with does, but gets easier with experience.

Using Cameras to Determine Age

You can also use trail cameras to pattern bucks on your property. There is no question about it. Serious deer hunters are using cameras to see what bucks are cruising near their tree stands and ground blinds. However, you can do more with those cameras than just see what is on your property. New research done by Dr. Mickey Hellickson shows how to determine the age structure of your herd and also pattern those big bucks. Let's first look at age structure.

There is no set rule on the number of cameras needed to determine your herd's age structure, but obviously the more you use the better. We would guess that one camera for every 50 acres would be super, but that might not be a number you can afford. Work with what you've got. No matter how many cameras you have available, your first step is to identify as many of the different bucks on your hunting area as you can using their unique antler and body characteristics. Examples of things you can use to distinguish your bucks are eye color, ear characteristics, the throat patch, drop tines, tall brow points, scars, burr points, anything that allows you to identify a buck.

Then assign an estimated age to each of these bucks using body characteristics (we've covered this in our *"Whitetail Advantage"*, Krause Publications, 2008). There are several books you can "Google" up on aging bucks on the hoof. It can be done.

Now you need to subdivide the age category of all the unique bucks into "young," "mature," and "old." Young bucks would be yearlings and 2½-year-old bucks. Mature would be those bucks that are large 2½s, 3½s and small 4½s. Old bucks are large 4½s and anything older.

You now have an approximate age structure for the bucks on your property. If you feel there are too many young bucks, then you need to modify your harvest to protect more young bucks. But you also need to be realistic. In Iowa, Hellickson estimates that it takes 500 acres to get one 5½-year-old buck. Still, you are shooting for as many mature and old bucks you can get, so manage your harvest according to what you found from your camera study.

One other thing. After

Several body and antler features can be employed to distinguish different bucks like this nice Florida ten-point with a uniquely-long brow tine on the right beam and the short G4 on the left beam.

your hunting season, you can use the teeth on the unique bucks you photographed, and then harvested, to see how good your photo-age-estimates were. Dr. Hellickson aged 13 of 25 harvested bucks correctly from photos, and another 10 within one year of their correct age. That's pretty darn good. He also estimated the score of each photographed buck and got seven of 28 right, and 12 of 28 within five inches. That ability apparently comes with lots of practice.

This is the same buck five days later. Even though it is facing away from the camera, the longer brow tine on its right beam and short G4 on the left verifies the identity of this buck.

Using Cameras to Pattern Bucks

Now let's move on to using cameras to pattern bucks on your area. First, get out maps, sit down with your hunting buddies, and establish permanent trail camera sites. There is no set number but obviously the more cameras out there, the better your results will be. One per 50 acres would be a good start. If budget restricts how many cameras you have, then rotate the cameras from one permanent site to the next. Put so many cameras out for two weeks, then move them to another site for two weeks, then move them back, etc. The key is to do this long term at the same sites, but make sure that you have the cameras at each site in use on the same time and date each week, each month, every year. Patterning bucks using cameras is a long-term deal. Several years of data sure beats one season of data.

Once you have determined where you want to place the cameras, put corn feeders there and start taking photos. Periodically, and yearly, you simply compare results from each camera site. Use the body characteristics described above to identify each buck. Okay, you can't identify every one, but with experience you will find that you can identify most individuals, and can even identify them from one year to the next.

Patterns will develop as you see that certain bucks are photographed at one site more than others. This tells you the approximate area where each buck is living. It might be useful to calculate the adult sex ratio at each camera site. Sex ratios will vary for each site. If a particular site has a lot of adult does, as well as a few mature or old bucks, then this information could be used to improve hunting success during the rut. Find the does and you find the bucks.

You also need to determine the percentage of bucks photographed during daylight hours for each camera site. Dr. Hellickson found that this varied on his Iowa farm, from zero to 70 percent. Some sites got no bucks in the daytime, other sites got a lot. (Where would you rather spend your valuable time hunting?) His average for daytime buck photos was 28 percent. The site that got 70 percent in daylight was a funnel area. Makes sense.

After several years you will start to see a pattern where big bucks are visiting certain camera sites, using some areas of your hunting territory more than others.

Hellickson found that most of the really big bucks harvested on his farm over the years were within 440 yards of the camera site where they were photographed the most. And the bucks that were photographed the most were the ones most likely to be harvested. Yes, on occasion they did harvest bucks that were never photographed, but most were killed near the camera where they were photographed.

Making notes on important habitat features at each camera site can also be helpful come hunting season.

Is it next to security cover? Are there funnels close by? Add it all up and you will come to one conclusion. The use of cameras where you hunt definitely increases your chances on bigger bucks. It does require some financial investment, but more and more hunters are using cameras and there is a reason: They work.

Obtaining a precise count of deer is difficult regardless the technique employed, but the collateral data such as sex ratio, age structure, fawn survival, and antler quality is extremely valuable information.

Knowing how many deer occur on your property is important, but knowledge of habitat and herd condition is paramount to a management program. Population estimates are required, but are no more important than the data collected following harvest.

If the average field dressed weight and antler dimensions of mature bucks in the harvest are above the county-wide average, or state for that matter, it is reasonable to assume that deer are in good shape. The collection of population and morphological data consolidated and compared annually represents a road map indicating where the program began and the direction it is heading. Thus the more information collected, the greater the chance of taking the right turn towards healthy deer herds.

(above) Minnosota resident Michele Leqve arrowed this 160-class buck in 2008 after first catching it on her trail cameras throughout the antler growing season in 2007. (Photo by Michele Leqve)

(opposite) Michele's buck first showed up on her cameras in 2007. (Photo by Michele Leqve)

(left) Capturing unique shots (note the moss on this guy's antlers) of whitetails in their secret world is difficult yet entertaining at times.

No one can deny the joy realized when reviewing pictures of our kids enjoying our favorite pastime as I (BZ) do with my daughters Nan and Beth. This was Beth's first deer.

IN THE EYE OF THE BEHOLDER: PHOTOGRAPHING THOSE BUCKS

The most precious memories for many sportsmen revolve around the time they spend outdoors with friends and family in pursuit of whitetail deer. Outwitting an elusive mature buck is a stimulating event etched into one's memory, but aspects of such experiences fade over time as sportsmen age and participate in other dynamic hunts in their lifetimes. A quality photograph or two can resurrect those sometimes forgotten events. No question, good photographs will allow you to relive those memories for years to come.

As college instructors, we often remind our students that a dull pencil is better than the sharpest memory and in reality this applies to photography. Even a poor quality photograph of a particular hunt is better than none at all.

For example, when we started hunting 40 and 50 years ago in the Appalachian mountains of Pennsylvania, we didn't give a thought to taking good photos of our early hunts. We were so overwhelmed by the simple fact that we were deer hunting that photographing our success just wasn't on our minds. Both of us

(left) Photography revital-izes those memories of friends and activities enjoyed early in life yet susceptible to be forgotten as we age.

(below) There is little one can goof up when filming an outstanding subject like this whitetail taken by archer Matt Rehor. (Photo courtesy Matt Rehor)

still vividly recall our first bucks, a yearling five-point (BZ) and a spike (DS), but we would give anything to have captured the wide grin on our teenager faces right after those hunts occurred.

Sportsmen and women enjoy a number of unique events throughout their sporting careers, and if cap-tured on film they can be revisited throughout their lifetimes, especially when no longer capable (heaven forbid) of being able to participate in the sport they cherish. For some, their success can be shared with family and friends—that is if that photo was taken cor-rectly.

The density of pixels making up an image is referred to as its resolution. The higher the resolution, the more information the image contains. For example, if we keep the image size the same and increase the resolution, the image becomes sharper. Therefore, with a higher resolution, a larger image can be obtained with the same amount of detail as a smaller one.

The take-home message is this: when selecting a new digital camera, buy one with the highest pixel rating that you can afford.

But remember, exceptional images can be obtained by using an affordable three pixel automatic camera that fits comfortably inside your pocket, as long as you're not interested in enlarging the print.

Another important feature of modern digital cameras is the sensitivity or ISO setting. The higher the ISO number, the less light required to capture a picture. More importantly, image quality is inversely related to the ISO number. The best images are obtained at or below 200. But there are times when a high ISO number is required, such as filming an outstanding buck right at dark. The image may not lend itself to producing an exceptional portrait-sized photo, but at least you have a photo.

Choosing a Camera

Taking a photograph is not difficult, but obtaining a quality image requires effort, time, and practice. The first decision one must make is to decide on brand of camera. Several companies produce exceptional cameras, and a variety of brands exist. Most all of them can capture quality images. Get on the Internet and research the various options, remembering that better quality is not always tied to expense. There are some great cameras available at economical prices. A quality camera is like an expensive well-tuned rifle. It has the capability to enhance one's ability to make that challenging shot, or capture that unique image.

We both started out using film cameras, but no sense going there. Today digital cameras have virtually replaced traditional film cameras. The major difference between the two is film purchases and development costs are eliminated as images are electronically recorded onto a card file situated in the camera body. And more importantly, the image is instantly available for review. There is no down time awaiting development. So if the shot is a little over or under exposed, it can be corrected on the spot.

Digital cameras are classified in terms of mega pixels, which equates to the number of pixels (short for picture elements) that make up an image. Pixels are a little like grain particles in a conventional photographic image, but are arranged in a regular pattern of rows and columns and store information somewhat differently. Today this number varies between one million (one mega pixel) to 14 million (14 mega pixels).

(above) Positioned correctly and shot with a shallow depth of field, the antlers are accented, and it is the antlers that are the focus of most buck photographs.

By simply repositioning the deer, a memorable portrait can be obtained. Note the antlers positioned above the hunter (BZ).

Photo Composition

Regardless of photography equipment, composition remains critical to collecting an exceptional image. For example, your hunting companion just shot a terrific buck. With all the excitement, you take a few photos right in the middle of the oat patch where the animal dropped. (Like we stated earlier, even a poor quality photo is better than none, but with a little effort, a more attractive image can be obtained.)

By following some general guidelines to field photography, an image can be captured that you are not only proud of, but that might be publishable.

First, reposition the

Photographs taken immediately following a kill are important, but with a little creativity, a descriptive picture of the event can be obtained, placing the viewer of the image at the scene.

deer near the brush line where the background accentuates the image. Position the lucky hunter behind, yet next to, the animal and elevate the antlers, if possible slightly above the sportsman. Never have a hunter sit on or stand above the animal

Remember, digital images are even less expensive, so take multiple exposures both vertically and horizontally at different distances from the subject. Take most of the pictures with the camera at a slight angle (approximately two to five degrees) below the subject.

Possibly the most important factor to consider when photographing a successful hunter is time of day. Mid-day photographs, when the sun is directly overhead, should be avoided. Light at this time is considered "flat" and the final image may be poor quality. The optimum time to obtain premier harvest shots is in the early morning and late evening hours when the sunlight is considered "soft."

On cloudy and rainy days or during the late evening hours when light

(right) Avoid positioning the hunter behind or above the rack as it interferes with the antlers, making the picture confusing.

(below) By positioning the hunter below and to the side of the deer, the antlers are accented against a blue sky.

(right) Taking images during mid-day should be avoided because the light is considered flat and shadows develop over the face of the lucky hunter.

(below) Most cameras come equipped with a flash that facilities late evening pictures and more importantly removes shadows during the mid-day period.

(bottom right) Composition is critical; what *not* to do is as important as what *to* do.

is limited, a flash should be employed. Flash is also a valuable tool in bright daylight when shadows pose a problem. Shadows occur in the later hours of the morning and early evening hours when the angle of the sun casts a shadow over the subject. Shadows can be eliminated by a technique referred to as fill-in flash. You simply take the photograph with the flash activated and the subject is highlighted and the shadows are eliminated.

Composition is critical to capturing a unique image. What not to do when composing a photograph is important. Some of the things to avoid include the exposed tongue of the deer or excessive blood on the animal. Whenever a harvested deer is filmed, respect for that animal is imperative so wash off the blood. We

know of a Manitoba guide (Big Grass Outfitters) that not only washes off all blood, mud, etc., but they then use a high-power blow drier to make the fur as life-like as possible. They take great photos in their camp.

Additional concerns are focused on the sportsmen. There is nothing less attractive than a deer held by a hunter with a cigar in the individual's mouth. It is an image that is less than attractive to the nonhunter, and these are the folks who unquestionably have an impact on our hunting future. Deer filmed in the back of a pickup are just as undesirable.

The depth of field or zone of focus must be understood in order to elevate a good photograph to a great one. Controlled by the F-stop of the lens, it is important to understand that the foreground—not the background—needs to be in focus. The larger the F-stop number, the greater the depth of field.

We prefer to shoot portrait shots of deer with an F-stop around f4.5 in order to blur out the background while accenting the deer's antlers in such a way that they jump out at you.

Vibration while taking a photograph ruins more images than any other factor,

(left) Even when a picture is taken immediately after the kill, all exposed blood should be removed. Also, be sure that its tongue is hidden. There is nothing more offensive than a photo of a successful kill with the tongue dangling from the animal's mouth.

(below) Accent the deer's antlers to make them jump out at the viewer.

(left) Use of filters can enhance colors of the image.

(below) Unlike conventional film, digital images are inexpensive, so take a lot of them and at a variety of angles and positions. You never know which one might be the most important of the group.

(left) Additional photos of activities surrounding the hunt should be obtained, so be creative. Photos tell the story.

(bottom) Sundown often provides an excellent opportunity to collect dynamic silhouette pictures.

making a tripod or some type of solid rest a necessity. Regardless of the quality of camera or lens, a quality image will never materialize unless the camera is held rock solid. It also facilitates the use of your camera's time release mechanism, enabling you to take that photo when no one else is around.

If possible, once the deer is eviscerated, place the animal on the floor of the cooler in a sternum position (feet underneath) and elevate its head slightly with a rope inside the cooler. The animal can then be transported back out into the field a day or two later under ideal lighting conditions, and filmed again. If available, use a set of glass eyes to enhance the animal's appearance (easily obtained from a taxidermist). With the lucky hunter situated slightly below the rack accented by a blue sky for a background, a dynamic, and more importantly, attractive image can be obtained. The blue sky can be enhanced further by employing a polarized lens filter. But remember, with digital it is easy to take numerous photographs. Probably the two biggest mistakes most deer photographers make on kill shots is 1) they didn't take enough photos at different angles, and 2) they were too far from the animal and the hunter. Fill the frame with animal and hunter.

(above) Although much of our time is spent focused on pursuing deer, some hunters spend hours in blinds, facilitating some great photo opportunities while awaiting that particular buck.

(right and opposite) The late, hot summer period forces deer to concentrate around water resources such as small ponds, windmills, etc. These are excellent opportunities to both film and scout for those big bucks.

Everything else is usually not needed. Regardless of the objective of taking a picture, performing these described tasks will increase the quality of images that you will be proud to display.

Taking additional shots of the successful hunter as he walks up to his quarry or drags it off adds another dimension to describing the experience to those viewing the pictures.

Harvest shots are important, but nothing is more challenging and rewarding than filming deer in the wild. Once again, background is important, so position yourself where a desirable setting exists behind your subject. A photo of a buck standing in a food plot is not going to stand out as much as it would standing in a pear flat or walking through the brush. Remember, the definition of photography is painting with light. Taking that unique image is an art form which takes practice, but is mentally and sometimes financially rewarding.

The rut is a great time to capture bucks on film as they drop their guard in search of does at this time, but most sportsmen are focused on hunting, not filming. However, with a little effort both activities can be accomplished.

Some sportsmen spend a substantial amount of time ensconced in a deer blind throughout the season observing lots of bucks, but not always the right one. By taking their camera to the blind, much of the down time can be converted into some unique opportunities capturing a number of bucks on film. After all, if you can film a buck, it's obvious you could have shot the animal, making a quality buck photograph a trophy in itself.

Sitting in a blind at sunset also affords sportsmen an opportunity to obtain unique silhouette shots of deer against a breathtaking view of an orange, pastel-colored horizon.

My (BZ) preferred time to film deer is during the late summer period when the animals concentrate around secluded water holes. At no time are deer more vulnerable to a camera than during the hot and dry summer period. A couple of hours of seclusion around your favorite water hole can provide some outstanding images.

Filming mature bucks, like hunting them, is not easy, thus camouflage is imperative. The lens on the camera is the paramount ingredient to a quality image. I (BZ) rely on my Nikon 400mm F3.5 lens because it not only yields impeccable images; it affords me a little distance from those elusive animals. My advice is to purchase as good a lens as you can afford, but stick with a 400mm lens if you intend to film wild deer. And be sure to employ the use of a tripod with these longer, heavier lenses. Obtaining quality images with a telephoto lens without a tripod is virtually impossible.

Filming summer time velvet-coated antlers is not only enjoyable, it can play a vital role in one's success later on during the hunting season. In reality, filming deer in late summer is another means of scouting, except you're documenting the potential trophies you see on film.

Filming your experiences in the great outdoors is the ultimate way to share those priceless memories with friends and family members. Why not do it right?

(below) Filming deer in the wild takes a lot of time and specific equipment, such as a quality telephoto lens and tripod.

(opposite) Filming deer in the summer doubles as valuable scouting time.

WATCHING A BUCK GROW OLD

Fawns remain close to their mother, but when they become separated their bleat call helps the doe relocate them.

The almost full-grown button buck fawn clumsily picked its way through the thick brush directly behind mom. Sometimes they would get separated, more common now that the fawn was rather independent, but a "bleat" from the fawn allowed the doe to relocate her offspring and they would continue on their daily journey. Once the verdant grain field was in sight, the careless fawn dashed under the fence and into the open field. The succulent oats were no doubt tasty, but the fact that the ubiquitous ticks and horseflies remained outside the clearing made it that much more desirable.

The fawn's mother hesitated for several minutes before entering, but once secure she glided over the barbed wire fence and into the field and immediately buried her head in the highly desirable food source. And so it was every day until the leaves changed color. Now the doe became a bit irritated with her fawn. Her behavior changed as the rut approached, and when the bucks started harassing her and mating occurred, the fawn remained with the family group.

It was at this time that he observed more humans in the woods. They wore orange-colored clothes and stealthily approached the fields. He'd seen people at various times in his first six months, and observing this activity would only magnify the inherent fear this deer had for man as it matured.

A year later, the buck had survived to the age of 18 months. Several biological changes occurred: a set of antlers developed on his head and, above all, he was sexually active. Winter came and went. Then spring, then the very hot summer.

Throughout the long, hot, sultry summer, the young buck bonded with three older bucks. The male companionship insulated the youngster from the many dangers in the wild as he imprinted on their actions. He was so attracted to the largest buck, a five-year-old 10-pointer, that his mannerisms almost mimicked this mentor. Following the older bucks, the youngster learned how to avoid humans by simply regulat-

ing its time around human activities. For example, a rancher would drive out and refill cattle troughs located at the windmills every three days with food. The older bucks' routine was to slip out from their protective coverts, following the rancher's and cattle's departure, and consume any remaining food left by the cattle.

Things began to change in the fall as the young buck noticed his older cohorts becoming increasingly aggressive toward each other. Although still accepted as part of the group, he was instantly subordinated whenever he did not follow their rules. It was mid November, and the yearling's sudden urge to pursue a doe was eclipsing his desire to eat. But the older bucks would not allow the youngster anywhere near a doe, particularly one in heat. He could tag along, but that was the extent of his first year of adulthood.

One particular foggy morning in the buck's second year, he watched as his mentor defeated another

(above) The jump can appear effortless, but it is extremely dangerous as they characteristically drop their back feet and get entangled within the top two strands of wire. This often leads to an excruciating death.

(top right) A buck develops its first set of antlers during its second summer and he can breed at that age. But his acceptance into the breeding hierarchy is constantly challenged by older dominant bucks.

(right) Young, submissive bucks often accompany older bucks until the rut approaches and the big boys get a bit more aggressive.

challenger for the rights for a particular doe. As the battle between the bucks ensued, the sound of an old truck could be heard in the distance.

Unlike exercising his normal, evasive response, the victorious buck, sporting a rack of huge proportions, remained stationary, almost statue like, in a semi-open area as the doe before him nibbled on a granjeno bush. The loud crack of a rifle removed something he did not wish to relinquish. The huge buck slumped to the ground, and the young buck ran a short distance away to watch the impact man had on his life.

Excuse any anthropomorphism we inserted

Each and every time a buck observes human activity it becomes more reclusive, sometimes to the point that it moves only under the protection of darkness.

(below) A whitetail buck faces the gauntlet of Mother Nature on a daily basis, reducing its chances of surviving long enough to develop a large set of antlers. The coyote has long been the number one deer predator in the South, but this predator continues to expand its range throughout the United States.

into this story, but scenarios such as this one happen often in the wild, and it's only normal that young deer repeatedly witnessing such events become extremely elusive. The fact is, wild deer are born with an inherent fear of humans, which is magnified by the number of confrontations the two have in the wild.

The intrinsically wild nature of deer is rarely subdued, even in penned animals. For example, in the late 1970s, I (BZ) raised wild whitetails in captivity for research purposes. Fawns were born to wild does bred by

Even with penned deer where fawns are removed early after birth and allowed to imprint on man, very few fully accept man. This buck was an exception. Most inherently remain shy around humans.

superior bucks in seven-to-ten-acre enclosures. During fawning season, pens were traversed daily to locate all newborns. Captured fawns were transported to a much smaller holding facility, enabling me to bottle-feed the animals. My objective was to develop a herd of tame deer, or at least deer that were imprinted on humans, thus more manageable. After conducting this project for several years, I discovered that some deer would actually become pets, while others failed to lose their fear of man, remaining wild and difficult to work with.

Deer in the wild are subject to an infinite number of intrusions while going through their normal daily patterns. Many factors, including hunters, automobiles, coyotes, dogs, and interstate highways, impact how long deer survive in the wild.

(left) Deer are inherently curious and sometimes show little fear of humans. However, as negative encounters occur, this behavior changes.

(below) Shooting deer from an elevated blind over a food plot is extremely effective, but when done too often, deer will shy away from such structures or quite possibly avoid them entirely during daylight hours.

rut is quite common. Now, is this coincidence or is it a learned practice? One could surmise that it is a direct result of the fact that the fewest hunters are in the field at this time. There is no way to prove this, but deer movements during the rut occur from 12-2 in the afternoon when many hunters are back at the cabin having lunch and a quick snooze.

It's obvious that in order for deer to survive, they must literally survive in man's back yard, and they are doing that quite well. But what about deer in the outback, where they live a more sheltered existence?

First, there are not many places where deer can live without encountering man. Deer almost everywhere interact with man on a year-round basis.

I managed a large Texas ranch back in the mid 1980s, which permitted little if any hunting. I leased the periphery of the 100,000+-acre ranch with the intention that the lessees would protect the core from poachers, thus deer in the core lived a sheltered life, at least from hunters. Not long after acquiring my responsibility as manager of the landholding, I solicited the help of my friend, then Assistant Professor Dr. Steve Demarais from Texas Tech University, to assist me with a study on mature bucks. By using telemetry, we intended to find out where mature bucks preferred to reside and how long they lived—vital questions to the trophy deer manager. In conjunction with the central theme of the study, individual buck behavior was also investigated.

One would think that visually relocating radio-collared deer would be easy—not so. The collared deer

It's important to note that deer are individualistic, demonstrating variable personalities. They are faced with predation by coyotes, dogs, hunters, or even collisions with vehicles. The point is, the animals must adapt in order to survive. Simply because a deer witnesses a fellow deer hit by a car doesn't mean it will never cross a road again. But the animal may very well avoid the road when the roaring sound of an engine is heard.

(above) By hazing bucks into a drive net with a helicopter, 25 mature bucks were radio-collared and monitored daily for four years on a 100,000-acre ranch. This allowed biologists to enter the secret world of the whitetail.

The same can be said about hunters shooting over oat patches. Shooting a few deer on a grain field does not mean that survivors will avoid the area. But you can rest assured that deer will alter their behavior around and on the plot, sometimes visiting only under the protection of darkness.

Deer have, for the most part, an uncanny ability to decipher when and where to make their appearances. Take, for example, the mid-day activity period during the rut. Based on results of research on radio-collared mature bucks, a mid-day activity period during the

made few appearances. As a matter of fact, one buck collared at 5.5 years of age survived to its tenth year, occupying a rather small area frequented by ranch hands. Yet, over the five years he was monitored, the huge buck was spotted only four times. It's important to note that the collared bucks were not disturbed except for the times we attempted to approach them utilizing the receiver.

This leads us to the question of how old do bucks live in the wild? There are records of deer living more than 20 years, but most of these deer were raised in pens under ideal conditions. Rarely do they survive over 10 years in the wild. In most public hunting states, in excess of 70 percent of their harvest is composed of bucks less than two years of age and less than five percent of the bucks reach an age of 4.5 years. Things in Texas are a bit different because most land is private and buck management is done to allow many bucks to reach older age classes.

Based on results of our telemetry work, the age of South Texas deer perishing from natural causes ranged from three to 10 years, and averaged 7.5 years. Our oldest buck was found dead in February, 1994, and he was nearly 11 years of age. This particular deer was in extremely poor shape and supported 98 inches of antler compared to 125 inches he supported at age 4.5 when he was initially captured.

Our largest radio-collared buck, nicknamed Double Main Beam, perished at 10; however, he was captured several months prior to his death and recollared and showed no sign of degradation. His body frame

appeared strong and his antlers of 189 inches were outstanding. Why he perished remains a question, but was probably related to an injury inflicted by another buck or bucks while competing for does.

The ultimate deer turf is composed of a land mass large enough to allow young deer to safely reach their older years. However, some older bucks utilize a very small area to bed and eat. Even for those old bucks other problems still exist. No matter how big or how small a buck's home range is, naturally-occurring mortality takes its toll. Like any living organism, deer do not live forever. Based on telemetry studies 15 to 31 percent of the bucks we monitored in Texas perished from natural causes on an annual basis. Another Texas wildlife professor, Dr. Charlie DeYoung, worked with a much larger sample size than we had, and discovered a natural annual mortality of 25 percent. If 25 percent of each age class is lost annually, it is not difficult to understand why so few big deer exist. Even with hunting excluded, it is difficult for the animals to survive the gauntlet of Mother Nature on an annual basis. Drought, coyotes, disease, highways, and even barbed wire fences

(bottom left) This 5.5-year-old buck nicknamed Double Main Beam was captured in 1984. It was observed only four times over the next five years. Amazingly he lived in an area heavily traveled by humans, yet still remained unobservable.

(middle) Double Main Beam at 6.5 years old in 1985. This buck was so elusive it was never observed on the annual aerial surveys, until a telemetry receiver was used to locate him from the helicopter.

(below) Double Main Beam at 7.5 years old in 1986.

(above) Time and cause of death of collared bucks can be determined by a mortality sensor affixed to each collar. Employing this technology, we found that the age of deer perishing from natural mortality ranged from three to 10 years.

(right) At 8.5, Double Main Beam was recaptured in 1987 in order to install a new battery for his transmitter. The magnificent animal gross scored a whopping 188 inches.

Surviving in the wild is extremely difficult for deer, but even when they do they can become their own worst enemies. These two apparently locked up during the rut while competing for a position in the breeding hierarchy.

take their toll on deer, making it increasingly difficult to feasibly manage for superior quality older bucks.

The most amazing thing I ever witnessed concerning deer behavior involved a yearling buck in a separate study on the same Texas ranch. Collared as a fawn, we had to relocate the yearling by helicopter to recover the animal for various research data. Once we isolated the animal's position based on the telemetered signal, we circled at approximately 75 feet above the ground. The buck never moved, so we retriangulated to verify the deer's position and hovered for several minutes 25 feet above the ground, but no luck. Convinced the deer died from some natural cause, we hovered over the area with the skids at times touching the blackbrush below us in an attempt to recover the collar. Seeing some open ground beneath the tangle of brush, I strained to find the collar. Failing to observe the color-coded collar, we prepared to leave the area when out from underneath the helicopter the yearling buck exploded. How could a deer, or any creature that young, refrain from running while a helicopter hovered over it for a sustained amount of time? Instinct? The point is, deer personalities vary, thus each one responds differently to the same situation. This individ-

ual variation in behavior may be the reason why deer have adapted so well and continue to grow in numbers.

Some students of the whitetail contend that there are unkillable deer. Deer that live a lifetime without contact with predators, man or beast. Whether it is some inherent trait enabling that animal to avoid disaster or simply luck remains a biological mystery.

From DNA data we now know that a few particularly large-racked bucks are so reclusive they don't even breed. They remain hidden and completely sheltered from interaction with man, and even other bucks.

(left) Older bucks are more evasive, but some young deer, even yearlings, can be elusive if not extremely reluctant to move when faced with danger.

(above) This particular buck, which would probably score in the mid 170s at seven years of age, was only seen once and this was in late January. He was spotted behind one of the most active places on the ranch where he lived—the shooting range.

(right) I (BZ) was privileged to film this deer three years in a row. He was never seen during the hunting season, but once it was over, he fed nightly in the cattle pens next to our ranch headquarters. He never displayed a broken tine.

I (BZ) have watched bucks that show up late after the rut is over without so much as a broken tine. One that comes to mind is a 29-inch-wide 12-point I was able to see over a three-year period. His antlers were so characteristic you couldn't mistake him. But he was quite reclusive, showing up at our headquarters pens when native forage was in short supply. Even in an area with a sex ratio slightly favoring bucks, the deer never had a broken a tine. Either he was one lucky deer or he was good at avoiding trouble, which is not the case with many of his broken-tined brethren in the same area.

If deer are so adept at avoiding man, how can hunters hope to shoot one of these bucks? The fact is, not all deer are the same. Some bucks, even the big guys, are rather vulnerable and predictable at certain times. I have witnessed two bucks sporting racks in excess of 190 inches that were totally predictable, but again, this was the exception and not the rule.

As for a buck that can be considered unkillable, it is possible. Deer that live inside the city limits are obviously safe from at least a legal hunter's bullet. And what about those nocturnal deer? Bucks that are either forced to be nocturnal like many east of the Mississippi where hunting pressure is extremely intense, or those that are just normally active at night, are at less risk from hunting. But even though nocturnal bucks occur, they are not found in substantial numbers, especially during the rut. With persistence and a lot of luck, particularly during the rut, that buck of your dreams may present himself. If not, enjoy the anticipation of seeing that monster, because it's the anticipation of what could step out that makes hunting just that—hunting, not killing.

ANTLER RESTRICTIONS: THE COMING TREND

E ven after fifty years, the heart pounded with antici- pation as I climbed up an old oak tree on opening morning. The weather was cloudy, but nothing would dampen my spirits. After all, this was the first day of another new bow season.

Eighty yards away a flock of turkeys left the roost and "putted" as they fed over the ridge. As daylight started to trickle through the trees, a migrating thrush took a rest just above my head. A few seconds later he flew off, but my attention turned to a patter in the leaves indicating an approaching deer. I slowly grabbed my bow and got ready. The buck walked directly under my tree, then quartered away. Normally, I'd harvest the first deer of the year for the freezer, but not this buck. Why?

I was in Pennsylvania and their new antler restric- tion law was in place. This buck had to have at least one antler with four points to be legal. He did not, so I passed him over.

In the past twenty years we have seen a huge inter- est in maximizing antler quality. Hunters want bigger bucks, at least many do, and so on private lands and leases they have adopted various strategies to get bigger bucks. They want to hunt bigger bucks, they enjoy using trail cameras to look for bigger bucks, they enjoy shed hunting for bigger antlers, they love watching videos and televi- sion shows about big bucks, and they will expend a lot of energy, not to mention money, to manage their farms, leased lands, and smaller properties for larger-racked bucks.

Forty years ago we didn't see this focus, probably because there just weren't that many deer out there. Hunters were satisfied to take any legal buck. But as

deer numbers grew, seasons and bag limits expanded, and does filled the freezer, an interest in bigger antlers started to bloom. About the same time we saw the growth of a non-traditional strategy of deer manage- ment known as quality deer management (QDM). Antler restrictions and increased doe harvests are two components of quality deer management. (As an aside, the third component is to eliminate the harvest of button bucks.) There is a national association that promotes quality deer management. The Quality Deer Management Association, headquartered in Watkins- ville, Georgia, is a 501(c)(3) non-profit organization founded in 1988 (www.qdma.org). Their objective is to educate hunters, managers, and landowners on how to practice proper herd and habitat management tech- niques to improve their property and hunting. They have over 30,000 members and dissemination of infor- mation is a major activity for this organization.

Map depicting membership growth of the Quality Deer Management Association. (Map compliments QDMA)

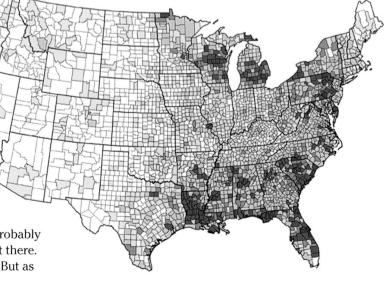

We (the authors of this book) really like quality deer management and what this group is trying to do because it emphasizes harvesting lots of does. In many parts of whitetail country, our forests have been ravaged by deer. We've lost many wild flowers, ground plant species, tree regeneration, ground nesting birds, and other components of the forest ecosystem. The key to resurrecting our forests and invigorating the habitat is to reduce our deer herds. If it takes putting antler restrictions on bucks to get hunters to take more does, we're for it. Apparently around the country more and more hunters agree.

Some people seem to believe that the Quality Deer Management Association started the idea of antler restrictions. Not so. Various states used some form of antler restrictions long before there was a Quality Deer Management Association. And QDM is much more than just managing for antlers. It is a holistic approach— habitat management and deer management. One aspect of habitat management is food plot development. We've seen a tremendous interest in building food plots. There are books, videos, television shows, etc., devoted entirely to building your own food plots. The Quality Deer Management Association supports antler restrictions if three conditions are met. First, they must be based on good data to insure that you are protecting most of the yearling bucks. Second, they must be accompanied by a monitoring program so that the harvest can be followed and changed when necessary. Third, hunters and landowners involved must support it. Do that and antler restrictions can help jump start a program to change the age structure of bucks and,

(above) The number one problem deer managers face today is an overabundance of deer characterized by a population skewed in favor of does.

(top right) Food plot management has become extremely popular with both managers and hunters. In drier parts of the country, some go as far as to irrigate these supplemental food sources.

(right) Harvesting does is the only way to control a deer population.

via doe harvests, get the sex ratio closer to something that makes biological sense. And since the sex ratio of deer at birth is equally distributed between males and females, a balanced adult sex ratio is closer to normal.

Another aspect of QDM is adequate doe harvests, and here again we've seen a huge jump in the harvest of does. And, we've seen more and more hunters coming to the understanding that if you want to improve the health of your deer herd and habitat, you need to harvest more does.

The key to bigger bucks is changing the age structure from yearlings to older age classes. On paper, that is fairly simple. First, let your young bucks get older. Don't shoot them. When you let young bucks walk, you end up with more mature bucks, thus, more competition for does in the rut, a shorter compact breeding cycle and more intense competition among bucks for does.

Some History

Antler restrictions are not new management tools. For example, back in the 1950s, in many states it was illegal to harvest a buck that didn't have one antler more than three inches long. But passing fork-horns or bucks with less than three or four points on one

(left) If your goal is bigger bucks, youngsters like this must be allowed to walk.

side is a relatively new management strategy that is being used more and more in various parts of whitetail country. In an effort to increase the number of mature bucks in the harvest, in the mid 1980s Colorado applied a three-points-on-one-side restriction in some wildlife management units, increased it in 1992, and by 1999 it was applied in all units. So they then decreased the number of buck permits and this resulted in more mature bucks. Since that time many states have experimented and/or adopted antler restrictions.

There are other ways to change the buck age structure. For example, if you reduce the bag limits for bucks you will increase buck age structure. Kentucky has done this with great success. You can also shorten the buck season, meaning fewer bucks will be harvested and more will then live to an older age. There are some other things that will change buck age structure as well, but we are just going to address antler restrictions because that is a major way of accomplishing that goal.

Let's quickly look at a succession of events that has brought us to where we are today relative to antler restrictions.

(below) If you pass up a fork horn like this yearling, it's highly likely he could be a six- or eight-pointer with a decent spread in his second year. And look out if he makes it to his third year.

Georgia

In 1993, Georgia became the first state to impose antler restrictions in a whole county. One such project was conducted in Dooley County, Georgia, by Micah Goldstein of the Georgia Pacific Corporation. He initiated a program where bucks had to have a 15-inch ear-to-ear spread to be legal. Apparently in Dooley County hunters cooperated in passing up such bucks. When they started in 1992,

A nubbin buck is a six-month-old buck with antlers barely visible.

yearling bucks made up 41 percent of the harvest. In 1995, that percentage had dropped to six percent. In 1992, only 20 percent of the bucks harvested were 3.5-years old, but by 1995 that had jumped to 57 percent.

This led to other counties moving to some form of antler restrictions, but the results have been mixed. As has been mentioned, when you restrict the harvest of yearling bucks you can expect hunters to take more does to fill their freezer. Older bucks are a bit harder to harvest, so hunters will then shoot does. At least that is the theory. When you impose antler restrictions on yearlings, you also expect the older buck harvest to increase.

In some of Georgia's wildlife management areas, the doe harvest did increase but the older buck harvest did not. Kent Kammermeyer and fellow biologists with the Georgia Department of Natural Resources suggested reasons that antler restrictions did not work were: may need more than five years for it to work on public lands, heavy hunting pressure around the boundaries of the public lands, buck dispersal from the areas, and high button buck harvest.

Mississippi

Mississippi was the first state to have a state-wide antler restriction in place. Mississippi has had a total of four point antler restriction since 1995. They allow the harvest of three bucks per year, but since they implemented the antler restriction doe harvests are up, and hunters like it. In fact, they have an 80 percent approval rating for antler restrictions.

When first implemented, 50 percent of all bucks shot were yearlings. The next year that dropped to 23 percent. Today, only 12 percent of the harvest is yearlings. This means that there should be more older bucks in the harvest. In fact there are. When implemented, 14 percent of all bucks shot were 3 ½-years-old. Today that is up to 27 percent. But there has been controversy. Research has shown that the average age of harvested bucks has risen from 2.1 years to three years. However, biologists at Mississippi State University have also found that, indeed, the average antler size for older bucks has decreased in some parts of Mississippi. They attribute this to "high grading" the best yearling bucks. For example, 2½-year-old bucks on one wildlife management area on the Delta scored 87 inches before the regulation and 78 inches after implementation. Obviously there is some high grading taking place. Thus, in 2009, they implemented a change from a total of four points to the use of inside spread. This new regulation will require more scrutiny by hunters before shooting, but it will protect 100 percent of all yearling bucks. However, Mississippi hunters are still very positive about antler restrictions and they are seeing and harvesting bigger and older bucks (even though those older bucks in some areas are not as big as they were prior to the regulation, there are more of them). Much to the delight of game agency biologists, antler restrictions in Mississippi have also led to the harvest of more does.

Arkansas

Arkansas has been running a three points on a side program since 1998. There you can harvest two bucks per year. Here again, the doe harvest is way up, while yearling buck harvest has dropped from 49 percent to 14 percent as of 2004. In 1998 Arkansas enacted a three-point-on-one-side antler restriction and today the buck harvest is down, the doe harvest is up, bigger bucks are being taken and most hunters support it.

The three points on a side restriction led to a buck harvest decrease of 41 percent from the previous year, but the doe harvest increased by 67 percent. We all know that hunters don't want to harvest more does, so they probably didn't like this new rule. Not so. A post-season survey showed that 76 percent of hunters still supported the new rule. And 87 percent said they were quite willing to give up the chance to shoot a small buck if it meant a better chance to shoot a bigger buck in subsequent years. But in more recent years there have been complaints about antler restrictions. Apparently a fair number of hunters do not care about trophy bucks and just want to hunt bucks. Even so, in 2009, antler restrictions in three wildlife management units in Arkansas went from three points on a side to four points on a side.

With four points on one side, this buck would be legal to harvest in parts of Arkansas.

Other States

Many states have since imposed some type of antler restriction in local areas. Most work to improve the age structure for bucks. New York is an example. In 2005 they began a three-year antler restriction program in two wildlife management units in southern New York.

At that time in the lower Catskills, most yearling bucks were either spikes or forked horns. So the antler restriction they imposed was that one antler had to have at least three points. The one exception was that hunters under 17 years of age could take any buck with one antler being three inches long.

In one of the wildlife management units for which there were data, when this program started in New York yearling bucks constituted 58 percent of the buck harvest. Three years later, it was down to 23 percent. The harvest of bucks 2½ years of age increased from 31 percent to 42 percent and the harvest of 3½-year-old-bucks and older increased from 11 percent to 35 percent.

There are hundreds of case studies showing that antler restrictions improve buck harvest quality and increase doe harvests. One example occurred on Chesapeake Farms on the eastern shore of Maryland. Before quality deer management was practiced on Chesapeake Farms, 58 percent of the buck harvest was yearlings and 22 percent were 3.5 years old or older. After QDM was implemented, yearling buck harvests dropped to 14 percent and old bucks increased to 54 percent.

The same result occurred on Gulf States Paper Corporation lands in Alabama. Gulf State manages many areas less than 1,000 acres, but using QDM on their lands the doe harvest increased, yearling buck harvests went from 57 percent to 30 percent, and 3.5-year-old and older buck harvests increased from eight percent to 24 percent.

Anderson-Tully Company (a large, private timber company) operates 250 hunting leases on their forested properties in Mississippi, Arkansas, and Louisiana. In 1987, they decided to implement quality deer management on over 90 percent of them. On their properties QDM seemed to work well, and from 1987 to 1997 deer harvest numbers remained constant, with an average of one deer harvested per fifty-four acres. During that period, buck harvest dropped slightly and doe harvest increased. Though fewer bucks were taken, buck size increased. In 1984-85, yearling bucks made up 70 percent of the harvest. In 1995-96 this had dropped to 32 percent. Over that same time span the harvest of bucks 2.5 years and older increased from 20 to 60 percent. Over that same ten years, not only did the average age of bucks increase (from 2.1 to 2.8 years), but live weights went from 136 to 163 lbs, and antler quality

One concern some hunters have for a minimal point count, such as the one used in parts of New York, is the fact that spike bucks are protected.

increased by 55 percent. Obviously QDM is alive and well on Anderson Tully timbered lands.

Getting bucks into older age classes, such as this large racked three-year-old, is one of the objectives behind antler restrictions.

International Paper Company began a QDM program in Alabama in 1990 with eleven hunting clubs in the program. By 1997 there were thirty-seven. During that time the percent of 2.5+ year-old bucks increased by 20 percent. Hunt club member support for QDM jumped from 50 percent to 73 percent. On another Arkansas site with nine hunting clubs participating, QDM led to a doe harvest increase of 50 percent (from one doe per three bucks harvested to one to one). Antler size doubled from 1991 to 1997. Hunter support for QDM was 77 percent.

In another study, Mark Thomas and Pat Minogue reported that from 1985 to 1991 there were 124 bucks harvested on a 3,350 acre tract in Alabama. Most were spikes and fork-horns. Then QDM was implemented and from 1991 to 1997 58 bucks were harvested, and all had eight points or better. Although buck harvest decreased under QDM, total harvest was about the same. Over the full 12 years of the study, 894 does and 182 bucks were taken.

Antler Restrictions Today

According to the Quality Deer Management Association, there are seven states that practice antlers restrictions for at least one buck statewide (Alabama, Arkansas, Delaware, Georgia, Michigan, Pennsylvania, and Georgia). The first state to do this was Mississippi in 1995, so this clearly shows that hunters are interested in antler restrictions. Fifteen other states have some form of antler restrictions in parts of their state.

Why the recent interest by states in antler restrictions? We feel there are two major reasons. One, agencies needed a way to entice hunters to take more does. Two, the quality deer management approach, which involves passing up small bucks and harvesting more does, has been gaining popularity on private lands in many states and this has led hunters to ask for more antler restrictions. Hunters see that quality deer management works and they want the opportunity to harvest bigger bucks.

Remember though, there is much more to antler restrictions than harvesting bigger bucks. Actually getting bigger bucks is only a small part of what antler restrictions are all about. In fact, the main objective of this management option is to get more does harvested. Harvest more does and you reduce the overall deer population. Reduce the deer population and you get healthier forests. With healthier forests, the deer (does and bucks) have better and more nutritious forage. Better forage and restrictions on harvesting smaller bucks means bigger bucks and a healthier herd. And giving hunters an opportunity to harvest bigger bucks means happy hunters, more willing to harvest more does. Yes, antler restrictions are being used to improve herd quality and buck age structure.

There are other ways to protect younger bucks from being harvested. One method used on private leases and smaller parcels of public lands around the country is to limit buck harvest to those having a certain minimum antler spread (see Chapter 19). This method calls for the hunter to make a visual judgment in the field. This method can be difficult and without an education process it is less than ideal for statewide programs. Thus, antler spread has not often used to implement statewide antler restriction programs. Instead, wildlife agencies have used a three-point or four-point-on-one-side as the minimum standard. However, as more leases (and the state of Texas) implement antler spread antler restrictions, watch for a growth in the use of antler spread as a way to protect yearling bucks from being harvested.

Antler restriction programs have not come easy. Critics believe that restrictions allow some of the largest 1½-year-old bucks (i.e., those with three or four points on a side) to be harvested. After a few years this might result in older bucks having smaller antlers than they normally would have in older age classes.

How effective are these programs? The key here is to have good follow-up research. Pennsylvania is doing just that by collecting data that will allow wildlife officials to tweak antler restriction programs to make them more effective. Arkansas and Mississippi are also collecting data.

There are various options a state can use to implement such restrictions. For example, in most places where restrictions are put in place, youth hunters are exempt. The reasoning is that limiting youth hunting may drive them away from the sport. Another example of a different approach to antler restrictions is being examined in Texas and Louisiana. They are both experimenting with a "slot limit" antler restriction. With this approach you can harvest the poor-antlered yearling bucks and protect other bucks until they are older. Hunters in many counties in Texas can only harvest bucks with one unbranched antler or bucks having an inside spread of 13 inches or more. Agency biologists feel this will protect bucks until they are 3.5 years of age. On 900,000 acres in Louisiana, hunters are restricted to shooting bucks that have both spikes less than three inches, or bucks with six or more points.

Texas utilizes a 13-inch spread minimum, and since this buck has beams that are inside the ear tips, he cannot be legally harvested.

It appears those antler restriction programs employing a four-point-on-one-side limit may reduce the antler size of bucks in older age classes—in other words, high-grade the buck herd. But the end result is still more older bucks with antlers larger than hunters are used to harvesting. This makes happy hunters and also stimulates increased doe harvests. If doe harvests continue to stay high and more bucks continue to

reach older age classes, watch for additional states to adopt antler restrictions as part of their management system. (For more on what has happened in Missouri and Pennsylvania, see Chapter 20).

The Quality Deer Management Association Position on Antler Restrictions

It seems that some hunters (actually lots of hunters) assume that "quality deer management" means "antler restrictions." To clarify this, the QDMA has listed three factors they use to decide whether they support mandatory antler restrictions. First, they want the antler restriction to be biologically sound meaning that it will protect a high percentage of 1½ -year-old bucks. Second, at least half of the hunters must support it. Third, there must be a good monitoring program in place to determine if the harvest strategy is working.

One further key and major point: Quality deer management is much more than antler restrictions. Antler restrictions are just one component of QDM. QDM involves harvesting more does and letting button bucks walk. It involves habitat management and getting the hunters involved in collecting data and keeping records. In other words, QDM is a program aimed at improving the quality of the deer herd and habitat, not just counting antler points.

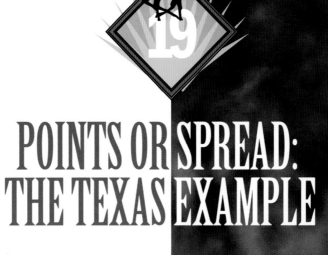

POINTS OR SPREAD: THE TEXAS EXAMPLE

When states started restricting buck harvests via antler restrictions, counting points was used as the selection criteria simply because it was felt that hunters could perform the task with less problems than judging antler spread. However, some biologists questioned whether this was the best method to protect yearling bucks from being harvested. In fact, data collected in Mississippi demonstrated that using the point method, hunters might be high grading (removing) the genetically superior yearling bucks, thus reducing the quality of mature bucks later on.

Even prior to the Mississippi work, Texas Parks and Wildlife biologist Bob Carroll was experimenting with antler spread instead of antler points as a way to protect yearling bucks. The width restriction most states use is ear to ear, which can vary from one region to another. In the North, such measurements are probably 18 inches, further south it may be 16, and in south-central Texas, where the first study was done, they used 13 inches. Thus if a buck in this portion of Texas had beams that lay outside the ear tips, it was considered 2½ years old or older. The general consensus is that antler spread protects yearling bucks much better than counting points.

The big question is, can hunters determine spread efficiently as they can count points? In 2002 the Texas the Parks and Wildlife Department imposed antler restrictions on an experimental basis in six south-central Texas counties. Their objective was not to create trophy bucks, but to improve the age structure of bucks in the deer herd. Of course since older bucks generally have larger racks, the result of improving the age structure of the bucks would be larger antlers. Additional goals of the experiment were to increase hunter opportunity and encourage landowners and hunters to become involved in managing the habitat. This experiment

With a 13-inch minimum spread requirement, this buck with antler beams inside the animal's ear tips would not be eligible to shoot.

was, however, a "slot limit" antler restriction. Hunters in six counties in the Oak Prairie region of Texas could only harvest bucks with one unbranched antler, bucks with one antler having six points, or bucks having an inside spread of 13 inches or more. Parks and Wildlife biologists felt that this would protect yearlings and 2½-year-old bucks. So this approach allows one to be able to harvest the smaller-antlered, less desirable yearling bucks and protect other bucks until they are older.

But could hunters judge the spread? With that problem in mind, the Texas Parks and Wildlife Department initiated an education program, using 400 posters and 50,000 pocket guides showing legal buck sketches. They also went into these six counties and conducted 34 public slide presentations to teach antler spread to hunters living there. Test photographs of illegal and legal bucks were shown before and after slide presentations with considerable improvements shown by hunters in judging legal bucks after completing the program. Apparently these educational programs worked because only 25 illegal kills were reported in 2004-2005.

Not only could hunters efficiently determine spreads, the antler restrictions employing antler spread improved the age structure in these Texas counties. Before antler restrictions were imposed, 80 percent of the buck harvest was composed of 1½ and 2½-year-old bucks. Within two years, harvest of 1½ and 2½-year-old bucks decreased to 45 percent. The percentage of 3.5+ year-old bucks rose from 16 percent of the harvest to 55 percent in two years. Hunters' support for the new antler restrictions was 72 percent. Even better, 70 percent of the hunters indicated that they enjoyed hunting more than they did before.

Things went so well that 15 Texas counties were added in 2005-2006. They modified the antler restrictions so that a legal buck was one with at least one unbranched antler, or a buck with an inside spread of 13 inches or more. As before, the idea was to protect yearlings and 2½-year-old bucks. And hunters made this strategy work. In 2006, in these 16 counties, yearlings made up 34 percent of the harvest, 2½-year-olds 25 percent, 3½-year-olds 27 percent, and 4½-year-olds 13 percent. In 2007, yearlings made up 26 percent of the harvest, 2½s were 22 percent, 3½'s jumped up to 34 percent, and 4½'s moved up to 16 percent. Thus, 59 percent of the bucks harvested were 2½ years old in 2006, but only 48 percent in 2007. In 2006, 40 percent of the bucks harvested were aged 3½ and 4½ in 2006, and 50 percent by 2007. Pretty impressive system!

By 2007 the harvest of 1½- and 2½-year-old deer in the original six counties was 28 percent, while 3½-year-old bucks represented 32 percent, and 4½-year-olds 41 percent of the harvest.

Forty counties were added to the program in 2006, and the latest word on the Texas situation is that 52 more counties joined the antler spread minimum in 2009, bringing the total to 113 counties employing this

(left) Now let's take a test. Review these six photos and, based on the Texas criterion, decide if the deer pictured are legal to harvest. With ear tips just inside the beams, this buck can be legally harvested.

(middle) Don't shoot—this yearling does not meet the Texas 13-inch spread minimum.

(above) Close, but this yearling does not meet the spread criteria so it should not be shot.

(left) Don't shoot — the ear tips extend out beyond the beams — great deer to protect!

(top) With beams extending out beyond the ear tips in the alert position, this buck is a shooter.

(above) Although this buck fails to meet the 13-inch spread minimum, it has at least one unbranched antler, qualifying it for harvest.

system. Watch for more and more states to go to this system of antler restriction. However, because some southeastern state have high numbers of spikes and the harvesting of spikes is a bit controversial (see Chapter 8), that portion of the Texas system may not be adopted elsewhere. But Texas has shown that with proper education, hunters can judge antler spread as a way of improving buck age structure.

However, note one thing. Just because we let a good buck grow older doesn't always guarantee the he will have superior antlers. Many years ago I (BZ) was crossbreeding deer in pens I had built on an East Texas ranching enterprise. I collected stock from the best ranches in South Texas and transported them to my facilities located not far from Athens, Texas. In an attempt to improve antler quality of the offspring, I carefully selected the best yearling bucks produced in our confined herds and bred them back to a number of does. The reason I did this was obvious. I simply assumed that the best-racked yearlings would produce the best or largest racks ultimately. What I found was astonishing because the best yearling I ever raised was an outstanding 11-point; however, he developed an eight-point rack in his second year and remained that way through his fourth year, when he was removed from the program. Thus, we must reiterate how unpredictable deer can be when it comes to antler development. It is not an exact science.

One must rely on the probability as to what can happen, and in most instances those bucks exemplifying good antler growth in their first year will more than likely be the ones producing the best antlers at and past maturity. Thus, let those young-racked bucks walk, and more importantly, propagate those desirable antler qualities.

A real clincher to the "let them walk" approach is the cruel realization relative to how many of those bucks you pass will reach those maximum antler-growing years. Number one on the list of concerns is the neighboring hunter. It's difficult to allow deer to pass by your stand when sometime during the season that animal will enter an adjoining property and never return. The answer to this problem is the consolidation of adjacent hunting tracts under the same rules and regulations. This has been attempted and successfully so in many parts of the country and the Quality Deer Management Associations Coop Program is really working. But in some areas that common trust among neighboring areas does not exist, thus eroding away any interest in following the rules. Of course, this new Texas rule guarantees that all landowners will abide by the 13-inch spread as a minimum requirement. They may require hunters on their property to take even bigger bucks than this minimum, but nothing can legally be taken that has a smaller antler spread.

We know that using a spread requirement works on smaller properties, but can it be effective on a county-wide basis? Based on the experiment utilizing spread as a harvest criteria in six south central Texas counties, it not only works, it has been accepted by sportsmen allowing them to enjoy the privilege of participating in the management of the whitetails they pursue, making their hunts even more memorable and rewarding. More importantly, Texas hunters requested these guidelines to improve their hunting experiences, and in a state like Texas where high fences are common, the ability of hunters to consolidate their efforts on open range is really refreshing.

This buck exhibited lots of mass and nine points as a yearling, but turned into an eight-pointer at 2.5 years of age and remained an eight-pointer at four years when he was released.

ANTLER RESTRICTIONS: THE MISSOURI AND PENNSYLVANIA EXAMPLES

A s interest in antler restrictions grew in this country, the use of this strategy to increase the doe harvest, and also the age structure of bucks, grew. We saw whole counties move to antler restrictions. We saw groups of counties move to antler restrictions. And in Pennsylvania we saw the whole state move to antler restrictions in what was to become a very controversial situation.

But before discussing that volatile Pennsylvania situation, let's move to a relatively recent development in antler restrictions (and what appears to be a much calmer situation): the one adopted and evolving in Missouri.

Antler Restrictions in Missouri

Missouri is an up-and-coming big buck state (see Chapter 14). Soon it will become even better, because they've implemented an antler restriction strategy. In 2004, to encourage more doe harvests in the high deer density counties, they implemented an experimental antler point restriction: antlered bucks must have a minimum of four points on at least one side to be harvested. (When you reduce the number of yearling bucks allowed in the harvest, doe harvests usually increase). The experimental period was for four years. There was mandatory checking in both the 29 experimental counties and 24 control counties where there were no antler restrictions.

After three years the Missouri Department of Conservation found that the doe harvest was three

With the requirement that a buck must have a minimum of four points on at least one side, such images are finished in northern Missouri. Allowing those youngsters the opportunity to age will provide larger-racked, older bucks for Missouri hunters to enjoy.

percent less than expected. However, if you divide the experimental counties into a moderate-density area (which was more agricultural area) and a lower density area (which was more heavily forested), and looked at the doe harvest, there was a difference. The doe harvest in the lower density area increased by 13 percent. Also, in the experimental counties, the yearling buck harvest declined by 66 percent. The harvest of 2½-year-old bucks increased by 56 percent in the experimental counties, but it also increased in the control counties. Thus, in the moderate-density areas only 16 percent of that adult buck harvest increase was attributed to the antler restriction regulation. In the lower density areas, 32 percent of the adult buck harvest increase was attributed to the antler restriction regulation. In 2007 the harvest of 3½-year-old bucks in the experimental counties increased by 62 percent. Overall, the harvest of all bucks decreased by 18 percent in 2007.

Hunter support was high where antler restrictions were in place. And there was even higher support (60 percent) after the four year experiment than before. One surprise was that in high deer density areas (mostly agricultural), doe kill did not increase. Even so, based on this 29-county experiment, Missouri has

decided to extend antler restrictions in 2009 to 65 counties. This means that almost the entire northern half of Missouri is under this four-point-on-a-side regulation. Apparently the southern portion of Missouri has lower deer numbers so there is not a push to put it under an antler restriction regulation.

This two-year-old eight-point is legal in Missouri.

In summary, antler restriction did what it normally does: it lowered the overall harvest of bucks, but increased the harvest of adult, older bucks.

Antler Restrictions in Pennsylvania

Every year, two to three hundred of this country's top deer biologists gather at the Southeast Deer Study Group Meeting. Both of the authors of this book attend this convention every year because it is the best way to learn the latest in deer biology and research. In 2002, one of the opening speeches was given by Dr. Gary Alt of the Pennsylvania Game Commission. He outlined the new and somewhat controversial proposals for deer management in that state. They were trying to increase the doe harvest and reduce deer browse, especially in forested habitats. "Society is looking to hunters to solve the over browsing problem that plagues our forests," Dr. Alt stated. He then outlined several proposals to increase the doe harvest, including the setting of antler restrictions. He noted their new antler restriction law whereby you could only harvest bucks with three points on a side or more in the forested regions of the state, and four points on a side in farm regions. His message was greeted with much support from the many deer biologists present.

No wonder. Deer biologists everywhere have long recognized the significant damage done by too many deer to our ecosystems. They were encouraged to find that a state was going to attempt to change that situation. The question was, would it work? Would the hunters, politicians, and Game Commission support it?

As just stated, Pennsylvania moved to antler re-strictions in 2002 because their habitats, their ecosystems where deer lived, were being destroyed by too many deer. Plain and simple, the Game Commission wanted more does harvested. In addition the buck age structure was a mess. At least 80 percent of all bucks harvested were yearlings. In some areas over 90 percent of the buck harvest was composed of yearlings. Plain and simple, there were very few older bucks in Pennsylvania. A change was needed.

Getting an antler restriction rule established did not come easy. Prior to adoption, Dr. Gary Alt, the deer program coordinator in Pennsylvania, gave over 100 talks around the state, explaining the purpose for the rule. His message was well received in some places, vehemently opposed in others. The system they had, whereby most bucks harvested were yearlings, had been in place for a long time and getting hunters to buy into something new proved to be difficult.

Part of the problem was that old timers grew up in an era where it was "bucks only" hunting, as the Game Commission tried to grow their deer herd. As they succeeded, a doe season was added, but it did not come easy. Many hunters resisted the killing of does, fearing that such management would "wipe out" the deer herd. There are still some Pennsylvania hunters that feel that way.

Then there were the younger hunters, those that came into the sport in the 1980s and 90s. They were used to seeing 20-30 deer a day, and although some of them originally supported the Game Commission's approach to lower doe density, by 2005, as doe sightings decreased significantly in some areas, that support waned and political pressure to lower doe harvests grew.

Remember, the whole idea was to lower deer numbers, especially doe numbers, and start the ecological recovery of Pennsylvania's forests. Before implementation of the new management strategy, it was felt that the hunters needed a carrot to encourage them to harvest more does. Antler restrictions create that carrot, plain and simple. Hunters were saying, we'll harvest more does for the opportunity to harvest

bigger bucks. That may be a bit of an over simplification, but it was the situation in 2002 in Pennsylvania. And so a three-points-on-one-side antler restriction was implemented in the heavily forested areas of the state, and a four-points-on-one-side was established in the agricultural areas of the state. It was felt that these restrictions would protect about half of the yearling bucks in the state.

In some areas of Pennsylvania, 90 percent of the harvest was composed of yearlings, a lot of them supporting small spike antlers.

Make no mistake about it, biologists and wildlife managers in other states were watching Pennsylvania. They had the same problems found in Pennsylvania: too many deer, damaged forest ecosystems, major losses of wild flowers and ground nesting birds, etc.

At the outset, 57 percent of Pennsylvania hunters supported antler restrictions, but others felt that there would be a lot of yearling bucks left dead in the woods. However, early on, things seemed to go well. Relatively few young bucks were found dead after the gun season, so that never really became an issue. After the 2002 deer season the ratio of adult does to adult bucks was high. In addition, there were not many mature bucks out there. The Game Commission captured a number of deer, but only two percent were adult bucks (2½ years of age or older). But results of the second year of Pennsylvania's antler restrictions showed

reasons for optimism. The 2003 doe harvests were the second highest ever with 322,620 being taken. And the buck age structure changed as well. Before antler restrictions, over 80 percent of all bucks harvested were yearlings. In 2003 buck harvest dropped by 19 percent statewide, thus more bucks entered the older age classes.

The state put radio collars on a number of bucks so they could determine what happened to them. In 2003, hunters took 66 percent of the 2½-year-old collared bucks. This told them that hunters were no longer killing all young bucks. Many older aged bucks were entering the harvest. In 2004 yearling buck harvest was down to 40 percent. This means that there should be more older bucks in the harvest. In fact, there are. When implemented, 14 percent of all bucks shot were 3½ years old. Today that is up to 27 percent. Not great, but an improvement. The buck to doe ratio was near two to one. Things looked good.

Well, not totally. Some things looked good. Others did not. For example, the number of hunters was dropping rather rapidly. From 1998 to 2005, Pennsylvania lost over 100,000 hunters. Some blamed the high doe harvest for the loss. That may have been part of the problem, but hunter numbers were dropping in many

(above) Some older hunters refused to shoot does. They believed that if you shot does, the buck population would suffer. That philosophy developed from a time when deer numbers were low and does were protected to grow deer herds.

(right) The chance for Pennsylvania hunters to harvest bigger bucks was the carrot the Game Commission hoped would encourage hunters to harvest more does in order to assuage the acute damage being done to forests.

states at this time. Not a good trend for the future of hunting.

There were other problems, with hunters complaining that the doe harvests were too large and they were not seeing deer. The trend continued in 2006 and by 2007, things were getting downright ugly. Hunters in some areas continued to grumble about not seeing deer. Internet sites buzzed with complaints from hunters. It seemed that most hunters liked the antler restriction, but they wanted to see more deer (i. e., they didn't like the fact that higher numbers of does were being shot in some areas).

And so in 2007 the Unified Sportsmen of Pennsylvania (a rather outspoken critic of the Game Commission for many years) filed a request for an injunction to stop all doe hunting on wildlife management areas and state forests until more data were collected on deer numbers. Let's look at the deer harvest for the past 10 years and see how it has changed (see Table).

More liberal doe harvests began in 2000-2001 and continued with the addition of antler restrictions in 2002. So, from the 2000-2002 seasons to the 2004-2005 season we see a much higher deer harvest in Pennsylvania. They were killing a lot more does. That's when things started going sour. The doe harvest was 322,620 in 2003-2004 and dropped to 226,270 by 2006-2007.

The reason for the decrease was because hunters complained and the doe allocations dropped, as did the harvest. There were also fewer does out there. From the buck age structure perspective, things continued to be good. Yearling buck harvest has dropped from as high as 90 percent to around 50 percent, meaning that hunters are harvesting older bucks, and larger bucks. But the overall harvests in the past several years are lower than they were in the late 1990s. Is this because there are fewer deer in Pennsylvania, or because the number of does allowed to be harvested has decreased? Hard to know. Probably both.

Table. Deer harvest by year in Pennsylvania from 1998-1999 to 2008-2009

YEAR	DEER HARVESTED
1998-1999	377,000
1999-2000	378,592
2000-2001	504,600
2001-2002	486,014
2002-2003	517,529
2003-2004	464,890 (322,620 of these were does)
2004-2005	409,320
2005-2006	354,390
2006-2007	361,560 (226,270 does, yearling bucks 56 percent of harvest)
2007-2008	323,070 (down 11 percent from previous year, 213,870 does, yearling bucks 56 percent of harvest)
2008-2009	335,850 (up four percent)

By placing radio collars on bucks, the game commission hoped to determine the impact antler restrictions were having on the male segment of the deer herd. What they learned was that hunters harvested 66 percent of the two-year-old collared bucks and fewer yearlings were being shot.

Almost assuredly politics has played a role here, which is nothing new in Pennsylvania. For many years politicians and hunter opinions have been heavily involved with deer management, much to the frustration of wildlife biologists trying to do their job. Things got so bad that in 2007 Dr. Gary Alt retired from the Pennsylvania Game Commission. The headaches of trying to lower deer numbers in Pennsylvania became too much of a personal burden.

The Pennsylvania Game Commission is like most state wildlife agencies. They need more money. But getting a license increase is very difficult when many hunters are upset that they are not seeing enough deer. In fact, this whole scenario is a catch 22. More data is needed on the antler restrictions approach, to justify progress and monitor results. But to get more data, the game agency needs more money. With hunters upset, getting such funding is going to be difficult if not impossible.

Probably in part due to political pressure, the Game Commission backed off on higher doe permit numbers and things have quieted down (a bit) since that time. Is the habitat still being hurt by high deer density in parts of the state? Probably. But what we are seeing in Pennsylvania is probably true in other parts of the country. Hunters are used to seeing lots of deer, and will complain loudly if efforts to lower those numbers are attempted.

Through it all, we do see support for antler restrictions that result in hunters seeing and harvesting bigger bucks. That's a given.

ANTLERS FOR SALE

Velvet removed from various antlered animals has been used for medicinal purposes in the Orient for hundreds of years. Prior to World War II, most velvet was obtained from Europe and Asia, but reindeer velvet from Alaska was exported to the Orient starting in the early 1960s. Soon thereafter red deer velvet was imported from New Zealand. Then later, a huge velvet production market developed via hundreds of deer and/or elk farms in the United States and Canada.

The demand for velvet continues today, but it is greatly curtailed due to chronic wasting disease. However, the Oriental demand for velvet is just one group (other than hunters) that has an interest in deer antlers. Many businesses want mounted bucks, and the bigger the better. Sporting goods chains, bars, sporting goods stores, sport shows, restaurants, and others all display big bucks. Bass Pro's Wonders of Wildlife Museum in Springfield, Missouri, has a great display of really big bucks. The Cabelas stores do as well and there are many other displays around the country. All such antler displays draw crowds, because people just like to see big antlers.

Google the word "antlers" on the Internet and you will get 3.3 million hits. Refine that search to "deer antlers for sale" and you get 250,000 hits, and the uses are varied and many. Jewelry, hand-crafted baskets with antler handles, handles for knives, lamps, chandeliers, buttons, door handles, gun racks, candelabras, chew bones for dogs, napkin rings, wine racks, and many other items are made from deer antlers. Then there are antler collectors who are constantly searching for the biggest, most intriguing bucks. These are people behind the scenes that collect antlers just the same as someone who collects antique cars or paintings. You don't know who they are or where they live, but they collect bone. The bigger and more unique, the better.

Then there are the shed collectors (see Chapter 6). Some shed

Those velvet-covered antlers are in demand for a variety of reasons other than hunting.

annual March auction in Dubuque, Iowa, one matched set of antlers went for $19,000. In 2008, the best set went for $4,500. Our friend, Kevin Wilson from Alberta, sold a matched set that scored 183 inches for $1,200. But many antler sets that score over 180 inches bring more. Huge nontypical antlers bring as much as $3,500, and those in the world record class may bring as much as $10,000. Legitimate antler collectors buy the big antlers, the unique antlers, and the ones that have an interesting history.

As with anything, the greater the demand, the more the item is worth, and this also applies to deer antlers. Of course, the bigger the antlers, the more rare they are, the more valuable they become. Thus, as with anything that is rare, theft becomes a problem. Google "stolen deer antlers" and you get 49,000 hits and lots of sad stories. You can read about antlers taken from live (then killed) bucks as well as dead deer at meat processing facilities waiting to be butchered. And of course many stories involve stolen mounted deer from private homes or taxidermy shops. There is also the occasional story of big bucks killed and antlers removed from deer being raised on deer farms and others stolen from hunting lodges. The stories go on and on, and in recent years there has been an increase in such activity.

A review of the Internet stories shows that hunters take some of these bucks. Most such stories where hunters took deer antlers involve only one animal. Some of these guys get caught later and the antlers or mounts are returned to the owner. But most stolen antlers are never found.

Then there are stories of heads stolen by criminals involved with all types of thefts, antlers being one. These involve some of the

(left) Antlers of all sizes are extremely fascinating to all.

(below) Antler creations from buttons to light fixtures are extremely popular items for the outdoor enthusiast.

hunters do it for fun (most of these folks are deer hunters too) and just want to find what kind of bucks are on their hunting lands. Others hunt sheds to sell them for money. In western states, shed hunting has become so big that a few states have gone as far as setting regulations on when you can shed hunt so as not to disturb other wildlife.

For those wishing to sell sheds, there is E-Bay and Craig's List, and there are also shed brokers who will buy antlers from you. There are also several major shed antler auctions held each year. No question though, shed hunting and selling is a big business.

For average sheds, a recent quote was around $12 per pound. Brown antlers seem to sell better than white or bleached ones. Fresher antlers also do better than older ones. And as we said, bigger antlers go for more than smaller antlers. For example, at the 2007

own exact duplicates of some of the world's biggest whitetails. Replicas are often found in traveling antler displays, but they are also purchased by individual hunters to place in their homes where they enjoy seeing them. For example, an antler artist and others helped Brian Andrews by recreating a duplicate of his stolen buck for him to have.

In fact, when state and national record bucks are harvested, some invest in a replica that can be transported to various sports shows for display. In that manner, they can show people the buck without the worry of someone stealing it. Some have gone so far as to put a replica on their den wall, while securing the

highest scoring heads. They are never found and the hunter has only a few photos to remind him/her of that hunt.

In 2003 young Brian Andrews bowshot a buck that scored 253 inches, making it the Iowa state record nontypical buck. In June, 2004, someone broke into the Andrews home and stole that buck. Since that time many huge Iowa whitetail mounts have been stolen from the homes of hunters. In late 2008, a reported 89 deer antlers were stolen from homes in two southwestern Illinois counties. One hunting club had 25 sets of antlers taken.

The high demand for the exceptional, world-class bucks, has led to a relatively new phenomenon: replicas. Skilled artists create molds and craft exact replicas of the original antlers using fiberglass. Then a taxidermist finds a hide and mounts the replicated antlers creating an exact duplicate of the original animal. The owner of the original real antlers gets a royalty for each replica sold. Creating replicas is difficult, time consuming, and requires a great deal of skill and training. However, for a price, anyone can buy and

(above) Shed antlers are used to make all kinds of hunting tools, from knife handles to rattling horns.

(right) Finding and analyzing shed antlers is an enjoyable pastime that can tell you quite a bit about the land you hunt and the bucks that inhabit it.

real antlers in a safe.

In 1993 Milo Hanson from Saskatchewan killed a world record whitetail. Those antlers meant a lot to Mr. Hanson, so much so that he reportedly turned down an offer of $150,000 for them. Many hunters turn down money for the big bucks they have harvested. Yes, regardless of how much some buck antlers are worth, for many hunters their antlers are just "not for sale."

(right) Shed antler hunters enjoy a variety of outlets to sell their antlers for a profit.

(bottom right) In some western towns, some businesses are dedicated solely to antler art.

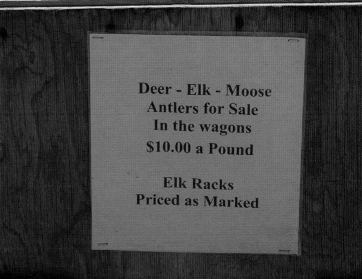

Deer - Elk - Moose
Antlers for Sale
In the wagons
$10.00 a Pound

Elk Racks
Priced as Marked

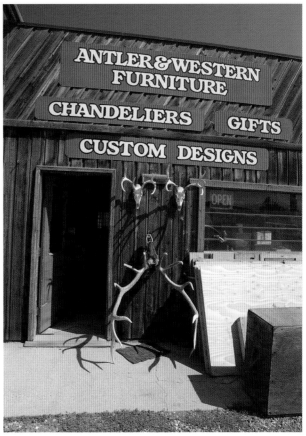

ANTLER & WESTERN FURNITURE
CHANDELIERS   GIFTS
CUSTOM DESIGNS

NEW AGE BUCK MANAGEMENT

T hings in the deer hunting world have changed. Just look at the differences one sees over the past twenty years. We have a plethora of hunting tools to use in hunting: range finders, new muzzleloaders, amazing high-quality clothing, all kinds of things to reduce human scent, an explosion in ATV's, field cameras, ground blinds, etc., etc.

Then there are the changes in deer management strategies. We've discussed quality deer management and antler restrictions and what that has done to enhance habitat in turn buck quality. But there are other changes: high fences, cloning deer, breeding big bucks, food plot technology, DNA research on deer, high tech equipment use in deer research, and more.

We don't know where all this leads us, but here are a few words on the changes we have seen in recent years.

Crime-Stopper Technology: DNA

In our previous book (*Whitetail Advantage*, Krause Publications, 2008) we covered this topic thoroughly. Rather than go over all that again, we refer you to that book. However, here is a quick summary of the research and the results accrued via the use of DNA.

Deer researchers are using DNA to answer questions about deer behavior that formerly had no answers. For example, using DNA we now know that around 25 percent of all twin fawns have different fathers. We also now know that most bucks only sire five or fewer fawns in their entire life. Through the use of DNA, we also know that yearling bucks do about one-third of all mating and that some old bucks do not participate in the rut. We've also found that there is tremendous variability in bucks mating does. Some small-antlered older bucks do a lot of breeding, others do little. Some large-antlered bucks do a lot of breeding, others do little. DNA tells us that and the DNA does not lie. The key man doing this interesting research is Dr. Randy DeYoung working at the Caesar Kleberg Wildlife Research Institute and over the next few years he will use DNA to unravel even more of

the mystery surrounding whitetail bucks.

High Fences

Driving through the Hill Country or the low-lying brush country of South Texas on a sunny morning, one can't help but notice the silver sparkle radiating from miles of high fence that is rapidly replacing conventional barbed wire fencing. Throughout the 1990s to the present, construction of high fences has escalated exponentially. And not just in Texas—they are showing up everywhere.

Why such an increase in its popularity? First of all, high fences allow managers to accomplish management goals quicker. Some individuals viewing a high fence surrounding a property for the first time often assume that it prevents access to the deer that belong to all of us. Certainly upon completion of a high fence, deer dispersal is curtailed. This fact alone makes management behind a high fence more challenging,

At one time we believed that only the larger-racked, older bucks did the breeding, but DNA technology provided evidence that yearling bucks such as this one do around 30 percent of all breeding.

Portions of this chapter came from Dr. Samuel's "Know Whitetails" column in Whitetail Journal.

because without the ability to disperse, deer numbers rapidly increase, placing much demand on the habitat. In other words, owners of high-fenced landholdings must control those populations to sustain a balanced population within the carrying capacity of the property.

Sportsmen are quick to point out that some landowners high-fence simply to keep their deer in. This is partially correct, but the major reasoning behind constructing a high fence is to keep deer out. That's right. By keeping deer from entering the property, the manager can control the deer herd, balance the sex ratio, even harvest bucks considered undesirable without deer from the outside moving in and negatively impacting all the hard work.

Some believe that big bucks exist behind every high-fenced property. That's just not true. As mentioned above, much more management effort is required within a high fence than out simply because the confined deer have nowhere to go to avoid poor, or worse, no management.

High fences represent a tool allowing landowners to intensively manage deer herds. They are effective and increasing rapidly across the U.S.,

(right) Although expensive and not applicable everywhere, aerial deer surveys represent a rapid means of collecting an abundance of population data in low brush country.

(below) New technology is being developed every day that allows us to learn more about whitetails. Employing a cannon net gun from a helicopter is both an effective and selective method of capturing big bucks in low lying brush.

representing one of the most controversial issues related to fair chase. One thing for certain, good or bad, high fences remain an integral part of the new age deer management era and their expansion has rapidly increased in the past twenty years.

Helicopters

During the South Texas fall and early winter, the drone of helicopters can be heard throughout the brush country as biologists attempt to assess deer populations prior to making harvest recommendations.

The helicopter is an extremely popular survey technique in South Texas, but it is not only expensive,

(top) In the early 1980s, highly skilled cowboys roped bucks that were hazed into the open with the helicopter. It was a time consuming process. Today with a cannon net propelled from a helicopter, researchers and managers can capture 100 deer per day.

(left) Wildlife management students from Southwest Texas Junior College collect appropriate data from a captured buck to be used as a sire in a temporary holding facility located on the ranch where the deer was captured.

(below) This series of photographs shows university wildlife management students releasing a 170-inch buck after collecting appropriate data.

its effectiveness outside the brush country is limited. But in Texas, helicopters provide a great way to count and review bucks (see Chapter 15) .

Helicopters are also employed to assist in the capture of deer for privately-owned high-fenced ranches. In Texas, a rancher can acquire a DMP (deer management permit) that allows owners of high-fenced properties to capture a particularly desirable antlered buck on their property and temporarily confine the animal, along with a maximum of 20 does collected from the same property, for breeding purposes. In other words, a buck demonstrating highly desirable antler qualities is permitted to breed a much higher number of does than it would in the wild. This also means that these does will not be inseminated by bucks with lesser antler qualities.

Additionally, a group of genetically superior does or a buck from a licensed deer breeder can be purchased and retained in a DMP pen, increasing the probability of developing some bucks that will demonstrate those highly sought after antler qualities.

Deer Farms

Today individuals owning as little as a couple of acres can obtain a license to purchase and raise whitetail deer. Not only is it popular, it can be lucrative as I (BZ) have witnessed the sale of individual bucks for substantial sums of money. But raising deer remains expensive. No question about it, some large bucks are being raised in pens, and subject to state regulations, they are for sale. The largest bucks are usually sold to other breeders as sires while others are sold to ranchers and farmers for release onto their property. Just a year ago, the breeding industry was touted as the most rapid-growing industry in rural Texas. Pennsylvania and Texas have the most breeding operations, but this activity is gaining a lot of attention throughout the United States, particularly by farmers and ranchers searching for a way to supplement their agricultural way of life.

Deer are being artificially inseminated in pens with semen collected from other huge-antlered bucks raised in pens from Mexico to Canada. A poor conception rate subdued this activity when it first started, but today a 75 percent conception rate is not uncommon when a group

Raising deer in confinement is done for various reasons throughout the country. Growth of such facilities for hunting has been limited in recent years because of chronic wasting disease. But raising deer for breeding purposes has grown in states such as Texas and Pennsylnaia.

Food Plots

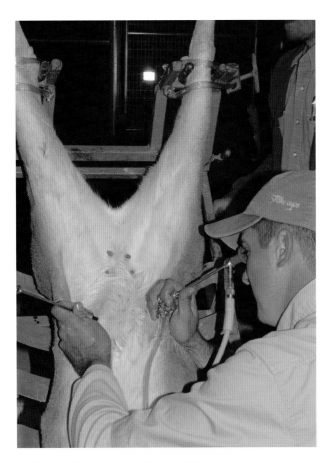

At one time, an oat patch was synonymous with a food plot. Not any more. The science and development of food plots for deer has taken on huge proportions. From a hunter with only 40 acres to land managers with thousands of acres, the use of food plots to enhance native forage has grown by leaps and bounds. Perhaps the ultimate use of food plots is the El Cazador Ranch in Texas where Dave Morris has intensively investigated the potential of food plots to grow big deer. Consider the following.

What if someone told you there was a 2,940-acre property that had a deer density of one per three acres and still harvested bucks with live weights averaging 218 pounds? What if that person also said that even with that extremely high deer density, the native vegetation is doing very well on this property? What if that same person told you that this was home to 209 bucks over 2½ years of age and that the top five bucks taken on that property in 2007 averaged 173 inches Boone and Crockett score?

Of course, your response would be that someone has been smoking too much weed, because none of the above is possible in the wild, right? Well, in this case you would be wrong, because there is one such place, the El Cazador Ranch in Texas, where the exception is the norm. How is it possible to grow so many big bucks on one area without destroying the native vegetation? For starters, at the El Cazador, they take food plots to the extreme and this ranch is a model showing what you can do with heavy duty plot management.

In 1998 David Morris purchased the El Cazador Ranch in Texas and soon joined with Dr. Gary Schwartz to develop an intensive food plot system for deer. Using 220 acres of food plots on 2,940 acres (that's 7.5 percent), their goal was to create enough healthy vegetation to totally replace native deer foods on the ranch.

The strategy was simple. Build large food plots (12 to 35 acres) to create more and nutritionally stronger food, and more and better deer. They didn't just want to attract deer to food plots, they wanted to feed them on the plots year round. Thus, they planted 135 acres of warm season plots and 85 acres of cool season plots. Their summer plots are mostly lablab and peas, and their winter plots are Tecomate Max Attract 50/50 and Monster Mix (a clover and chicory blend) (www.tecomate.com). Though there are year-round plots, the high protein summer plots are the key to their success.

Normally when you get high deer numbers (and one deer per three acres is an extremely high density), the native habitat suffers. But Morris created enough food via plots to feed high numbers of deer and create large bucks. Dave determined that a one-acre Tecomate food plot would feed three deer and he used that formula to create his plots.

To go along with their extreme food plot system,

of doe are laproscopically inseminated. Deer are even being cloned, but the chance that huge bucks will be duplicated and released in the wild are about zero. It's too expensive and will have little, if any, impact on wild deer. Consider that approximately 70,000 whitetails are registered in Texas by licensed breeders. With an estimated three million deer in the state, breeder deer represent only .018 or 1.75 percent of the wild population.

A 75 percent conception rate is not uncommon when a group of doe is laproscopically inseminated.

Disease in licensed deer breeding facilities is always a concern. Although respiratory disease (pneumonia) and EHD, blue tongue, are responsible for a high percentage of deaths, the number one killer of deer in pens is stress. Managers of deer breeding facilities work closely with veterinarians to combat the various diseases that whitetail contract. In order to prevent the spread of chronic wasting disease (CWD), deer 18 months of age or older upon death are required to be examined for its occurrence. If discovered, all inhabitants of the facility are dispatched. Even so, the spread of CWD in northern states has been directly linked to the transportation of deer and elk from one facility to another. CWD on game farms is one thing, but the subsequent spread to the wild is a major concern to state wildlife agencies. That is why many states have imposed serious restrictions on the interstate sale and movements of deer and elk from one deer farm to another.

they also distribute supplemental feed as a safety net during drought. Deer do not eat a lot of supplemental feed on the ranch because the native habitat is in good shape, but it's available all year long. They estimate feeding each adult deer ¼ lb. of cottonseed with minerals per day.

They manage for a balanced herd and maintain 1.6 bucks per doe sex ratio. (That's right, there are more adult bucks on the ranch than adult does. They only want enough does to replace losses.) Prescribed burning is also conducted, and they also manage for grasses and weeds to provide fawns escape cover from coyotes.

The results of this unusual and intensive management approach are rather amazing. But there is no question they have augmented the quality of deer. Let's look at some comparisons of their deer herd in 1998 and 2007. Total deer numbers were 1,231 in 1998 and 942 in 2007. Boone and Crockett average scores were 129 in 1998 and 150 in 2007. The number of mature bucks recorded in 1998 was 53 and 209 in 2007. Clearly Dave Morris is doing something right on El Cazador, and he believes this can be done on smaller tracts of land.

But there is a downside: it is extremely expensive to perform such extreme management. Such plot and habitat management is very expensive and labor intensive. In fact, it is estimated that running this intensive program costs in the neighborhood of $45,000 a year. Clearly this isn't for everyone.

Native Forage Enhancement

In recent years we've also seen a great deal of new work being done to improve native forage. This enhancement can be defined as the art of manipulating native habitat to augment the nutritional quality for all wild inhabitants, including whitetail deer. Native forage enhancement (NFE) is based on the successional stages in plant development. Whenever vegetation on a particular area is disturbed by activities like fire, disking, tree thinning, etc., it reverts to an earlier stage of development referred to as secondary succession.

An example of secondary succession is abandoned crop land, a common sight in agricultural regions, particularly one previously forested. No longer maintained, the area becomes inundated by grasses and other herbaceous plants. In a few years these same grasses and weeds are replaced by brush species such as blackberries, sumac, and hawthorns, providing excellent food for deer and cover for cottontails. Many years later, this plant community is shaded out by the canopy of a mature forest.

This orderly and progressive replacement of one plant community by another until a climax community occurs is referred to as ecological succession. Armed with this information, sportsmen desiring to improve deer habitat can implement a strategy in which the various stages of plant growth beneficial to deer can be established and maintained.

The advantages of NFE are many. First of all, you work with native vegetation. No seed purchase is required. You deal with vegetation deer are not only used to consuming, but often desire most. NFE can be conducted virtually everywhere you hunt. It can be performed without the use of tractors or any of the other expensive equipment used to establish conventional food plots. Thus it can

The roller chopper is just one of the tools employed to reverse the successional stage of vegetation in dense brush. Referred to as sculpting the brush, habitat manipulation practices are conducted in a well-thought-out design.

be performed in difficult, hard-to-get-to places. It also requires no fencing. Remember, NFE is the attempt to enhance the growth of native vegetation.

Cameras

The development of motion detection cameras is rapidly gaining in popularity because not only can one obtain population data, but scout for a big buck at the same time. These cameras simply represent another element to deer hunting as sportsmen can enter the secret world of the whitetail year round. More importantly, it's fun. We now have the knowledge to know how to place cameras on property that allows one to 1) get an idea of the number and quality of bucks on the property, and 2) know where to put a tree stand that will allow the harvest of those good bucks.

Conclusion

Indeed big buck hunting is changing rather dramatically. Never in our history have we seen the interest and the success hunters now have in harvesting mature bucks. But the technology is also changing. Take Maxbo 727 as an example. This is a yearling buck on a deer farm in Texas that scored 264 inches. You read correctly, a yearling that scored 264. Great breeding and great food has led to this unbelievable yearling buck.

Some of the changes in this new era are a bit frightening. But most of them enhance the management quality of all deer and enhance hunting opportunities as well. Whether you agree with all of them or not, they are here to stay. In 1985 there were 14 million deer in this country. In 2005 that number jumped to 30 million. Clearly that many deer has an impact on habitat and man. But times are changing relative to harvest. Consider that 1999 was the very first year we ever harvested more does than bucks. Relative to deer management, that was a huge accomplishment.

With the quality deer management strategy leading the way, we are starting to see more mature bucks enter the harvest. In 1999 the percent of yearlings in the harvest nationwide was 51 percent, but that dropped to 45 percent in 2005. According to the 2009 Whitetail Report put out by the Quality Deer Management Association, Pennsylvania yearling buck harvest dropped from 80 percent to 52 percent from 1999 to 2005. Wisconsin's dropped from 68 percent to 51 percent and Mississippi saw their yearling harvest drop from 50 percent to only 12 percent. Clearly we are entering a new era in deer management and buck harvest.

It's a bit hard for us old timers to fully fathom all the changes that are taking place in the world of the whitetail. With everything we've covered in the preceding pages, it is obvious that today's buck hunters are living in a new age for white-tailed deer. We encourage you to take advantage of the opportunity to get into God's woods and enjoy the outdoors with family and friends. We'll see you there.

This buck showed up on a privately owned three-acre tract of land in central Florida—pretty cool. Over the coming years you will read a lot more about using cameras to enhance your buck-hunting opportunities. There is a whole new science developing around cameras, and you are the beneficiary.

unting season is over and, for many, so ends the best part of the year. However, there are hundreds of thousands of us who keep deer in our hearts all year round. When snows fall, we walk the woods looking at deer trails, wondering which bucks made it through the hard times. What bucks will we see on our trail cameras this spring? How big will their antlers be this fall? For us, the appreciation and respect for the white-tailed deer never ends.

Spring is time to hunt sheds, a time to reconsider where our tree stands were placed last fall. Once examined, we move them to new locations in anticipation of the coming hunting season. Oh yes, we also move those trail cameras around, and get the equipment and seed ready for food plot planting. Then comes the summer when evenings are family time, with binoculars checking the fields to see just who is out there this year.

Did "split G2" make it through the winter, and how big is he this summer? What about "Double Brow Tine" and "twitter?" And then comes the fall, the velvet drops away, the antlers are full grown, and bow season is near. We've been shooting, the stands are set, we have some idea who is out there, and it is almost antler time.

The hunting is fine. The appreciation even better. Nothing means more to the hunter than seeing how "split G2" or "twitter" or a myriad of other bucks look this fall. We may not see them, but we know they are there. The rubs and scrapes tell us so. Maybe a trail cam photo confirms it. And that is enough.

Sure, a harvest would be great. But it probably won't happen, and we move on, sitting, watching, and appreciating what we have in the outdoors. Soon, another fall hunting season ends and another antler season begins. Life is good.

ANTLER SEASON NEVER ENDS

Once the season is over, the anticipation of next season begins.

DEER &
DEER HUNTING
MAGAZINE

PRESENTS

Shop Deer Hunting.COM

Providing
you with the
knowledge you
need to become
a better hunter!

Get the best deals around on:

- Books
- Calendars
- Videos, CDs and DVDs
- Online Courses
- Magazine Issues

New products being added daily!
Watch our weekly newsletters for updates.

PLUS! ...save an **extra 10%** on all
purchases when you join the Deer
& Deer Hunting Insider Club.

Save
25-30%
on many
products!

www.shopdeerhunting.com